I PRAYED AND NOTHING CHANGED

WHAT GOD IS UP TO IN THE SILENCE

Ste Casey

New Growth Press, Greensboro, NC 27401
newgrowthpress.com

Names and identifying details have been changed in vignettes and stories shared, except where permission has been given.

Cover Design: Studio Gearbox, studiogearbox.com
Interior Typesetting and eBook: Lisa Parnell, lparnellbookservices.com

ISBN: 978-1-64507-221-8 (paperback)
ISBN: 978-1-64507-222-5 (ebook)

Library of Congress Cataloging-in-Publication Data

Names: Casey, Stephen (Pastor), author.
Title: I prayed and nothing changed : what God is up to in the silence / Stephen Casey.
Description: Greensboro, NC : New Growth Press, [2024] | Series: Ask the Christian counselor
Identifiers: LCCN 2024020165 (print) | LCCN 2024020166 (ebook) | ISBN 9781645072218 (print) | ISBN 9781645072225 (ebook)
Subjects: LCSH: Prayer—Christianity. | Trust in God—Christianity. | Suffering—Religious aspects—Christianity. | God (Christianity)—Faithfulness.
Classification: LCC BV220 .C37 2024 (print) | LCC BV220 (ebook) | DDC 248.3/2—dc23/eng/20240513
LC record available at https://lccn.loc.gov/2024020165
LC ebook record available at https://lccn.loc.gov/2024020166

Printed in India

29 28 27 26 25 4 5 6 7 8

"Honest about struggle, unafraid of tough questions, realistic about life's challenges, and yet hope-saturated, Ste Casey fights to help us see more of Christ, even when we feel like he's silent."

Amy Smith, Resource writer; podcast host, *Faith in Kids*

"Here is strong encouragement for when we experience that most heartbreaking of issues—seemingly unanswered prayer—from someone who knows this experience very well. I wish I had read this before tragedy struck in my life and God didn't answer my desperate prayers in the way I wanted."

Marcus Honeysett, Director, Living Leadership; author of *Powerful Leaders: When Church Leadership Goes Wrong and How to Prevent It*

"It seems so unnatural and unfair to us to embrace weakness and sit in suffering, trying to believe that God is hearing you and doing something in the silence of unanswered prayer. However, in this book, Ste wonderfully shows us through personal experience and biblical rigor that God is working in the waiting—he is giving grace in the suffering and he is strength in our weakness. A wonderful, thoughtful, and hopeful book for all who pray and feel like nothing is changing."

Steve Robinson, Senior Pastor, Cornerstone Church, Liverpool, UK; director, Cornerstone Collective; dean, Grimké Europe; author of *Serve: Loving Your Church with Your Heart, Time, and Gifts*

"This book deals with a vital but overlooked topic. Drawing on his years of pastoral experience, his own story of suffering, and the apostle Paul's account of his thorn in the flesh, Ste has given us a wise, warm, and easy-to-read resource that transforms our perspective and turns lives around. I am so glad I read it and I want others to do the same."

Andy Robinson, Training Director, Living Out; training director, South Central Gospel Partnership, UK; former pastor

"In this succinct but powerful book, longtime pastor Ste Casey tackles head-on the experience of disorientation and disillusionment we often face in the wake of persistently unanswered prayer. What is God up to amid our weakness and waiting? Written with pastoral warmth and rich biblical insight, *I Prayed and Nothing Changed* points the reader repeatedly toward the sufficient grace of Jesus Christ at work transforming us in our darkest and most hopeless places."

Michael R. Emlet, Faculty and Counselor, Christian Counseling & Educational Foundation (CCEF); author of *Saints, Sufferers, and Sinners: Loving Others as God Loves Us*

"In the agonizing experience of unanswered prayer, we long for a wise and compassionate companion to walk with us. Filled with honesty, drenched in grace, and so powerfully personal, this book is that companion. It will be a blessing to many, particularly because in regard to unanswered prayer, Ste Casey is not just a faithful guide but also a fellow traveler."

Steve Midgley, Executive Director, Biblical Counselling UK

"This book is powerful and practical, making a very helpful contribution to a common human experience. Ste helps us to see what we don't always want to see about who God is and what he is up to when it seems as though he is doing nothing. This book is gritty, honest, and relentlessly practical. I highly recommend it."

Peter Sondergeld, Lead Pastor, Restoration Church, Toowoomba, Australia; pastoral and counseling supervisor; author of *Becoming You: Becoming the Person God Made You to Be*

"This precious book answers an often-asked question, but it does so much more than that. Ste draws us into the kind, loving, sovereign heart of a heavenly Father, a selfless Savior, and an all-able Spirit. He grounds this counsel deeply in Scripture and connects it to the messiness of life that we all see and feel. I'm better off for reading it—better in myself and better equipped to serve others who are telling me, 'I prayed and nothing changed.'"

Adrian Reynolds, Pastor and Head of National Ministries, Fellowship of Independent Evangelical Churches, UK; author

For my younger brother, Andrew,
for whom we prayed and nothing changed.
We miss you.

To my six precious daughters:
when you are weak, then you will be strong.

CONTENTS

Chapter 1

HE WORKS

"God is a distant stranger to me right now," Derek said as he wiped a tear from his face. His assessment of his relationship with God came after a long discussion of what was troubling him. A likable young man in his twenties, Derek was struggling. He remembered a time when the motivation for simple tasks was easy and enjoying church and worshipping Christ came naturally.

But since facing the big disappointment of a relationship ending suddenly, he didn't feel able to apply himself to anything. The life he had hoped for was slipping away before his eyes, and the God he had trusted seemed asleep at the wheel. My heart went out to him as I saw the confusion and sadness that were wearing him down. He didn't want to feel so spiritually forsaken. Yet here he was, facing unwanted circumstances and hurts that were crowding out any sense of the Lord's goodness and grace. Hearing the name of Jesus, rather than lighting him up and lifting his burdens, left him feeling dejected, forgotten, and guilty.

As he finished explaining his struggles, I offered to pray that the Lord might help him find a breakthrough.

It's an instinctive and loving thing to do—to expect in faith that the Lord will be present and working, even at the bleakest times. After all, Christ came into the world to seek and to save the lost. We all come into his kingdom when we are most aware of our need of the Savior. He meets us with grace, working behind the scenes with mysterious providence, preparing our hearts to accept his personal grace toward us.

But I'll never forget the look on Derek's face and the change in his posture when I offered to pray. His shoulders dropped and, with disappointment written all over his face, he simply said, "I've prayed and nothing changed." A strange mix of despair, confusion, resentment, and dying hope were heavy upon us both in that moment. Circumstances had come upon him and experiences had marked him, jolting him into a painful awareness of his weakness and producing an unwanted, soul-unsettling state of intense vulnerability. Yet when he cried out for relief, help, anything—silence. It only compounded his pain.

You know how he feels, don't you? While you might not have said it to me, you've probably felt something similar, haven't you? You've been at that point where something you were desperately wanting—urgently pursuing—is slipping away from you or is not coming into your life. Something precious—a relationship, your health, the health of a loved one, a career, a dream—is slipping away. Everything is falling apart. You can't see the future, and you've said, "Lord, I do love you, but if you're going to show up, now is the time to do it." You prayed and you prayed, and you prayed and you prayed. You said, "Lord, I'll do anything; just change this."

A week goes by, a month goes by, and a year goes by . . . still nothing seems to change.

A few months ago, I had a very honest conversation with a pastor friend. He'd been through some very difficult circumstances, and more stuff was coming at him—trouble that had been brewing for years. I asked, "How is this seemingly unchangeable struggle, which seems to be getting worse, affecting you spiritually?" He said, "Ste, I never thought I would say this, but it's affecting my ability to pray about everything." He didn't want to stay hopeless, but his experiences and the lack of answers were doing something between him and the living God. He didn't like it!

I've spoken with countless people recently who are wondering whether the change they desperately want will ever come. A mother desperately praying for a change in the diagnosis of her terminally ill son. A teenager passionately praying that fickle friends won't leave him sitting alone during his lunch break again. An exhausted wife earnestly praying that the Lord would save her marriage. An addict praying for release from the slavery of needing just one more. A husband pleading for the soul of his unconverted wife. A depressed retiree longing that the Lord would restore to him the joy of his salvation. So often the change we think we need, so clearly defined in our mind, so reasonable a thing to ask, seems far away from us. It hurts, it leaves us with questions, and we wonder whether God cares. Why won't he give us the change that we seek and feel we need?

Have you ever been there? I suspect you have. It's a strange double sorrow. Not only have you not received the change that would deliver you to a better place, but also you feel let down, even abandoned, by the living God. If this is your present reality, I realize how painful the encouragement to reach out again in faith and hope might be to you.

Perhaps you can identify with the brutally honest words of C. S. Lewis as he reflected on the emotional roller coaster he and his wife Joy experienced, as they tried to face her cancer diagnosis with faith and hope.

> What chokes every prayer and every hope is the memory of all the prayers offered and all the false hopes we had. Not hopes raised merely by our own wishful thinking, hopes encouraged, even forced upon us, by false diagnosis, by X-ray photographs, by strange remissions, by one temporary recovery that might have ranked as a miracle. Step by step we were led up the garden path. Time after time, when He seemed most gracious, He was really preparing for the next torture.[1]

When we open Scripture, we find that C. S. Lewis was not alone in experiencing intense periods of loss and questioning. This experience is echoed and amplified throughout the Bible. Wow, God is even admitting to us that unanswered prayer is a real thing!

- We all know the tragedy and atrocities that overwhelmed and crushed Job. He spent days pouring out his complaint, in desperate faith, seeking understanding and renewed hope in the Lord. But he never got the change or answers he longed for.
- The psalms, where we process the best and worst realities of life before the covenant-keeping God,

are jam-packed with rich, joyful communion with God. Yet, as Tim Keller points out, "There are, however, even more psalms of complaint, cries for help, and calls for God to exercise his power in the world. There are also stark expressions of the experience that God is absent."[2]

- Of course there's the most famous unanswered prayer, coming from the lips of the Lord Jesus Christ himself, as he knelt in Gethsemane crying out to his Father that the horrors awaiting him would pass from him—asking if there was some other way (Matthew 26:39, 42). Three times (Mark 14:35–41) the agonizing plea was sent heavenward to his Father, the same Father who had earlier in the Gospel declared, "This is my Son, whom I love" (Matthew 3:17; 17:5; Mark 1:11). Yet, on first glance, it would seem that God the Son himself knows what it means to pray and find heaven unyielding.
- And then there is the pleading of Paul that the thorn in his flesh would be removed. Rather than the answer he wanted, he got the exact opposite. The thorn remained, ensuring that he walked with a limp for the rest of his life.

Scripture speaks with vivid, personal stories that, on first glance, appear to offer us nothing more than the conclusion that the living God has sold us fake news about himself. Rather than being gracious and powerful, he is unwilling or incapable of answering our prayers. End of story. God is not working.

Sadly, that was the sentiment of my friend Derek. When he uttered the words, "I prayed but nothing changed," it was more than a statement of fact; it was a disappointment-laden declaration about the character and power of God. He isn't powerful, he isn't present, and he can't be trusted with the precious things of my life. End of story; God is not working. But is that really the case?

PAIN AND DISAPPOINTMENT NARROW OUR GAZE AND SHRINK OUR WORLD

On a recent vacation, traveling through the French Alps, my usually tech-addicted daughters had all in unison laid down their devices in order to squash their faces against the minivan windows to catch a glimpse of the staggering vista that was opening up before them as we descended the mountain pass. Audible gasps, followed by cries of "Look at that, Daddy, it's beautiful" and "You've got to see this" filled the car. They were caught up with a vision of the grandeur and awe-inspiring beauty that surrounded them. But not me. I didn't have the capacity to focus on anything other than the terrifying problem that had unexpectedly become an urgent concern.

The steering wheel in my hands was beginning to shake violently with each attempt to turn at the next steep hairpin bend. With ten more miles of steep winding descents ahead of us, it seemed that the brakes were overheating and failing fast! As adrenaline kicked in, my mind could focus on nothing but the problem. Minutes earlier I had been planning our next stop, thinking about what we would be doing the next day. That was gone. Moments earlier I had been joining the girls in enjoying the beauty of what surrounded us. That was gone. The only things I could see, think about, and feel were the calamity coming at us around the next bend, my powerlessness in the midst of our current situation, and the near impossibility of surviving the next few minutes.

Given that you are now reading my account of our journey, it goes without saying that we made it through and got the mechanical assistance we needed to continue safely. Though I could bore you with the details, I would rather let you in on what I have reflected upon many times since that experience—that unwanted and intrusive circumstances have a way of so hijacking our attention, emotions, and focus that the larger vista gets crowded out. When we struggle with unanswered prayer, it's easy to become so preoccupied with what God isn't changing that we lose connection with the gracious ways he is present and powerfully at work in those unwanted and painful seasons in life.

Pain and disappointment have the ability to narrow our gaze and shrink our world to the size of what's bothering or interrupting us the most. In our weakness, we're blinded to anything other than relief. Fixing what is wrong so dominates our thinking that we are prone to miss what's right in front of us, especially the often intangible realities of the always-present grace of God. It is in him that we live and move and have our being (Acts 17:28). He is the biggest player in any given moment, yet he drops out of our spectrum of vision. This is not to minimize the duration or intensity of your struggle but simply to point out that when our bandwidth is jammed up with merely getting through the day, it can be difficult to see the bigger story that will actually help us get through the day.

Author and pastor Jason Meyer presses this even further when he contends that the Christian life is primarily a fight for sight—a fight to be able to see beyond the current moment and all the questions it brings to a God who is bigger and doing bigger things than we can often see. He says, "We lose heart when we buy into the lie that our difficulties are bigger than God; we lose the fight for sight when we fail to see God correctly. When perception and reality don't align properly, it is easy to become discouraged."[3]

If Meyer is right, and I think he is, then that changes the way that we face the moments when it seems that our prayers are not changing anything, that it is the end of the story, and that God isn't working.

Think about how Meyer's perspective causes us to reconsider again each of the scriptural examples of unanswered prayers. On first glance, regardless of the specific person involved—Job, the psalmist, Paul, or even Christ himself—and taken in isolation from the story that they were a part of, they seem hopeless. Yet not only was it by no means the end of the story for any of these praying people, but also it was a hugely significant part of the story. Even saying that isn't quite strong enough or shocking enough. The experience of "I prayed and nothing changed," as unsettling and unwanted as it seems to be, is a vital part of the Lord's dealings with his people. It brings discoveries of grace and mighty revelations of God's goodness to his people.

FIGHTING FOR SIGHT

Outrageous as it may sound, we need to consider the possibility that unanswered prayer, and our experiences of it, may be a vital part of God's gracious dealings with us—even a doorway to some new experience of his grace and glory. Yes, it's shocking and terrifying, I know.

For that reason, as Derek dwelt in despair, I was cautiously smiling on the inside. Not with some sadistic glee at his misery, but because I could see that rather than this being the breaking of him and his faith, in the organized plan of a gracious God who meets us in the middle of all our struggles to redeem and renew, things were about to get exciting. My task was to walk with him to help him lean into the Lord as he experienced all the things the Lord *was* doing at a time when it seemed like the Lord was doing nothing. This was going to be a fight for sight—a fight to see that while he was waiting, God was working.

Unsurprisingly, Derek was going to take some convincing. Perhaps you know how he feels. Could there be a place in Scripture where one of the Lord's people was so assailed by a life-dominating loss and weakness, which was casting a dark shadow over every moment and every future possibility, that he despaired even of life? Could it be that he pleaded and pleaded for it to be removed, yet nothing changed? And could it be that as he looked back upon the experience, even boasting about it to others, rather than it breaking him, through the Lord's grace it was making him? Well, there is such a story. And this will be our focus as we fight for sight to see things the Lord is doing at the moments we most fear he isn't doing anything.

> Therefore, in order to keep me from becoming conceited, I was given a thorn in my flesh, a

> messenger of Satan, to torment me. Three times I pleaded with the Lord to take it away from me. But he said to me, "My grace is sufficient for you, for my power is made perfect in weakness." Therefore I will boast all the more gladly about my weaknesses, so that Christ's power may rest on me. That is why, for Christ's sake, I delight in weaknesses, in insults, in hardships, in persecutions, in difficulties. For when I am weak, then I am strong. (2 Corinthians 12:7–10)

The second letter to the Corinthians is the most personal of Paul's writings, and, for me, the most difficult to come to terms with. I'm glad I'm not alone in thinking this. A pastor recently whispered to me in hushed tones that of all the books of the Bible, it was the one he least wanted to believe and follow. It is where all the seeming paradoxes of Scripture are concentrated and let loose. We learn from Paul that in the kingdom of the crucified and risen Lord, surrender is success, weakness is strength, and humility is greatness. There is no joy without pain, no victory without wounds, and no wealth without loss. It is where the great apostle, who wrote one-third of the New Testament and was arguably used more for the cause of Christ than anyone else in history, is the most honest about his weaknesses and frailty. It's not easy reading, particularly for someone like me who is highly committed to having a self-sufficient and comfortable life.

Paul shares, with brutal honesty, his struggles. He talks about how he prayed three times. We're not talking about once at breakfast, once at lunchtime, and once at dinner. No, we're talking about a prolonged period of time because of agony that has lasted fourteen years. That word he uses, "thorn," is closer in meaning to "spike" or "javelin." It is something that was so excruciating and so debilitated his life that he wasn't sure whether he could go on. It pierced deeper than his body, into his very sense of who he was, how he was going to live, and what he was going to face. Day after day it weighed him down. It wore him out. It exposed his limits. It literally crippled him. It affected him physically, emotionally, and spiritually.

People have debated for centuries what this "thorn" was. We don't know exactly what it was, but we do know that it floored him. Christians throughout church history have taken up and used the motif of a thorn in the flesh to put words on circumstances and situations that have afflicted them and exposed limited prospects of overcoming these situations. We do know for sure that it made Paul weak. This is the great apostle! He prayed and he pleaded, and I wonder whether his heart sank, like Derek's, when it happened for a second prolonged period. I wonder whether he began to ask questions like "Is the Lord really good? I'm working for you here, Lord; if you fixed this one thing, I would be able to serve you better . . ."

Yet, as he recounts these struggles to the comfortable and power-obsessed new believers in Corinth, what echoes even more loudly is an unshakable confidence in the work of God for his people in, and through, regular disappointment and pain.

THE PROMISE OF ALL GOD'S WORKING

More than thirty years ago, freshly having come to know Christ as my Lord and Savior, I learned my first Bible verse. In it the apostle Paul speaks of the magnitude of a change that the living God is working in his people: "Therefore, if anyone is in Christ, the new creation has come: The old has gone, the new is here!" (2 Corinthians 5:17). Paul wanted to reinforce to the church in Corinth that God's redeeming love in Christ changes everything.

Paul's own story demonstrates this. Raised in an intensely religious tradition, he used the name of God, while in reality he worshipped at the altar of strength and self-righteousness. As he traded on the name of the living God without actually knowing him, Paul made himself an enemy of God. Paul's pride and spiritual presumption led him to rationalize all kinds of cruelty to Christians, leaving Paul feeling smug in his self-sufficiency and worshipping at the altar of his own importance. It was spiritual treason of the highest order that left him, however ignorant, dead in his sins.

But because of God's great mercy, Paul was literally stopped in his tracks. Three times in the book of Acts the story is recorded. The living God invaded his life with the person of Christ, who had paid the penalty for his treasonous sin, and broke the power of death at work within him. Paul was a new creation "in Christ." He had a new identity—as God's child—that trumped all others. He had a new purpose—to live to the glory of the God who had called him. He had a new command—to give himself away for the sake of others being brought to Christ for the glory of Jesus's name amongst the nations. He was a new creation—all God's doing and all a gift of grace. All of this was achieved not by the worth of Paul but in the life, death, and resurrection of the Redeemer Jesus Christ on Paul's behalf to the glory of God. Or in the words of Paul in 2 Corinthians, "All this is from God, who reconciled us to himself through Christ . . . not counting people's sins against them" (2 Corinthians 5:18–19).

When Paul entered the Christian life, he came with nothing, he came needy, and he came helpless in need of grace. This is the only way any of us can receive grace. God gives his redemption to those who are willing to admit they need it. This is the gospel hope that Christians bet their lives upon.

But the grace was not over; the grace continued through the process of God working to make Paul into what he was already in Christ. This is the difference between being and becoming. What Paul now was (being) —by the grace of Christ a new creation—the Lord promises to work out in Paul's life (becoming). Jerry Sittser explains this better than I can:

> Redemption promises to transform us—completely so. Once broken, we become whole again; once selfish and insecure, we become stately and serene and self-giving; once rabid sinners, we become glorious saints. In short, God purposes to claim us as his own—no matter how far we are from him, how fallen into sin, how lost and lonely. He wants to restore us to right relationship with him and to remake us according to the image of Jesus Christ, which will ultimately lead to the renewal of the whole world.[4]

What a vision—a Redeemer for everyone who will come! This is the promised work of redemption that the Lord was tirelessly accomplishing in the life of Paul. Paul's part was to trust and receive, to believe and pray, as his redemption and renewing played out in his life.

THE PROCESS OF ALL GOD'S WORKING

More than thirty years after first memorizing that verse, I am beginning to come to terms with what it really means for me to be going through a redemption process. I remember praying that verse, asking that the Lord would work out the fullness of its promise in me. Maybe you have prayed similar Bible verses for personal change and usefulness in the service of King Jesus. You too have longed to get from A to B, if A is a new creation in Christ, and B is the full-grown version of it. But I hadn't grasped the discomfort of the journey from A to B. It is a long journey of walking with the Lord, sometimes on the mountaintops, but often through dark valleys. That process is littered with pain. I want the fullness of the promise—I want the payoff—but fight him all the way on the process. So many of my prayers are pleas that the Lord would deliver me from the process. "Lord, give me relief from this thing that you are doing in my life! Change this now!" Yet the process is the whole point.

Though I may be surprised that pain and struggle are part of his process, the apostle doesn't seem to be at all.

> We do not want you to be uninformed, brothers and sisters, about the troubles we experienced in the province of Asia. We were under great pressure, far beyond our ability to endure, so that we despaired of life itself. Indeed, we felt we had received the sentence of death. But this happened

> that we might not rely on ourselves but on God, who raises the dead. (2 Corinthians 1:8–9)

We rightly see a horrifying diagnosis, a debilitating accident, a wayward and self-destructive child, or a relationship going south as a terrible affliction or obstacle, but in God's hands these things are another occasion to enjoy deeper fellowship with and dependence upon him. If redemption promises personal happiness or the good life as we imagine it to be, then we have a right to be angry and disappointed with God, for he will have failed us. But redemption promises a new heart and holiness, which are much more enduring than worldly happiness.

His redemptive work is not just to rescue us *from* something, but to rescue us *to* himself. As C. S. Lewis observed,

> God designed the human machine to run on himself. He himself is the fuel our spirits were designed to burn, or food our spirits were designed to feed on. . . . God cannot give us happiness and peace apart from Himself, because it is not there. There is no such thing.[5]

My tendency, because of my love of ease and my sin-sick heart, is to fight God all the way on this. But as life comes at Paul and flattens him, he sees it not as an assault of a callous and indifferent God, but as a time of expectancy. While he is waiting, the Lord is working. Paul expects that the Lord will be working, and has already been working, for a deliverance within him greater than he could ever imagine—a moment to refocus his hope on the redemption that was being worked out for him by the Lord.

Today, I worked with a rake on my lawn. It would have been easier to leave it alone, given the mess that it makes and the distress that it causes to the grass. Yet, I do it because I know what unseen terrors are hiding below the surface seeking to sap away its life. I'm talking about weeds. Though I may be tempted to rip the lawn out and replace it with artificial grass, I instead chose to work patiently, often gently and sometimes with more vigor, to rid my lawn of all that would rob it of life and steal its intended glory. As I labored, it occurred to me that my heart is much like that lawn. My sinful tendencies toward self-sufficiency and self-righteousness run deep, robbing me of the life Jesus has won for me and the glory that is due to him. My heart needs a gardener to work it—patiently, often gently, but on occasion in such a fashion as to force a showdown with the sinful weeds that dwell inside of me. The promise of his work is that I will be remade into the image of Jesus by his Father the gardener (John 15:1–4). To this end he works, personally and patiently. But on occasion the process might require some raking.

Even as I type that, I feel terribly torn. I love the promise, but everything within me recoils from the process. Perhaps that reveals how much I find the precious words of the Lord to Paul in his time of need so difficult to truly believe for myself: "My grace is sufficient for you." So tender and monumental, yet just not what I want to hear. When you feel stuck and alone in the process, the promise feels far away and, dare I say it, even unimportant.

But the high point of faith for your soul, when it struggles, will be to cling by the tips of your fingers to that hope—hope that your unanswered prayers, rather than being the end of the story, are a vital part of the story that the Lord is working in your life. As I once again invited Derek to turn with me toward this active God in prayer, I knew that the invitation wouldn't answer all his questions or solve all his problems. The pain, doubt, struggle, and temptation to unbelief would not disappear in an instant, but his prayer would be a fight for sight—to see past the current pain and disappointment to One who was present and working. In vulnerability, could he risk shifting the focus of his prayer from a prayer for doing or getting to something much closer to his Father's heart—a prayer for being and becoming?

I'd like to invite you to do the same as we journey with the apostle through his own personal experience of "I prayed but nothing changed." Perhaps right now you can see nothing but darkness and feel nothing but despair. Behind the veil of sorrow and confusion, through the experience of waiting, there is a God of sufficient grace. Will you ask him for sight, not mere understanding, but to see him in a way that changes your heart in the midst of your struggle? An enormous shift in a soul can happen in an instant as you stand in his presence. Rather than measuring God's faithfulness and grace by what he does for you, you begin to cherish what he is doing in you. Through his Son he is available to you right now. It is certainly true that while you are waiting, he is working. But he is also waiting, waiting for you to come to him for grace for today.

A DAILY PRAYER FOR SIGHT

Father, Son, and Holy Spirit, I confess that your grace doesn't feel sufficient for me today. My sight, my mind, and my eyes are clouded by my troubles. I'm worn down with all the unanswered prayers. Would you do what I can't do, and give me grace to sustain me and those I love this day? Would you give me eyes to see even a glimpse of what you are doing in the midst of my disappointment and powerlessness? I want to believe that while I am waiting, you are working, even if I can't see it right now. Teach me to pray and to not lose heart. I ask these things in Jesus's name. Amen.

Chapter 2

HE KEEPS

I appreciated the moment of honesty. She said, half with anger and half with deep sadness, "Keep me? It feels more like he's killing me!" I was talking with a young lady, Lisa, who had been struggling with her singleness for a long time. A number of times, she had a relationship that seemed to be working, but either she said or did something wrong, or the guy she was with just wasn't the right one. She was beginning to wonder, *Is this my lot?*

She'd heard it said that it's better to be left on the shelf than to be locked in the wrong cupboard, but right at that moment, being locked in the wrong cupboard was looking more appealing than life as it was. She was deeply saddened that she couldn't find somebody to share her life with—someone who would be with her and care for her.

Many of her friends were getting married, but those weddings, where she was supposed to be happy for her friends, were moments of real sadness for her. She came to speak to me, trying to find a way through the struggle, and as you'd expect a pastor to do, I asked, "How is this affecting your spiritual life?" She was honest: "I've prayed about this for so many years now, and I can't understand why God doesn't hear me. Doesn't he know what this is doing to me?" Of course, if you try to bring in spiritual wisdom and counsel too early in a conversation with somebody who is struggling, you invariably will say the wrong thing. And I did exactly that! I said, hopefully more gently than this, "The Lord is going to keep you through whatever your future holds, and right now, the Lord *is* keeping you."

That's when I heard her say this: "Keep me? It feels like he's killing me."

And there it was, a raw cry of desperation and accusation—a version of which may be the very reason that you have chosen to read this book. She had ridden the roller coaster of prayerful hopefulness and was now facing the chilling reality that our dreams for life do not always come true. It felt like a death. Why won't God bring his power and potential in line with our solution to our pain—in line with what we want? That's the kind of keeping power we are so often looking for.

CAN YOU BE KEPT AND KILLED AT THE SAME TIME?

It was plain that Lisa couldn't see a way that both could be true—being kept and being killed at the same time. It seems unthinkable to consider that the Lord, in his eternal graciousness toward us, might be doing more for us by giving us less of what we want him to give. We find it hard to grapple with the notion that there are worse things that can happen to us than unanswered prayer. Yet the apostle, as he shares his experience of very urgent, but unanswered, prayer with the Corinthian church, invites them to believe that the very thing he had prayed to be taken out of his life was being used for the greater purpose of keeping him for eternity. In the same way, we are invited not just to trust that he is always keeping us personally but even to pursue hope and comfort in that. Sometimes God, in unanswered prayer, is doing more for us than we can imagine. Sometimes his refusals keep us from deeper regrets. Sometimes there are worse things that could happen to us than unanswered prayer. God is not rejecting you, though it feels like it at the time. No, he's not rejecting you; he is *protecting* you! Not every pain is a punishment. Perhaps we need to consider how the pain from which we want relief is the Lord's way of keeping you close to himself. This is certainly how Paul begins as he recounts his own experience of that phrase, "I prayed but nothing changed": "To keep me from becoming conceited because of the surpassingly great revelations . . ." (2 Corinthians 12:7 ESV).

A large part of our agony when facing unwanted situations is in the uncertainty of the outcome. The key difference between a tragedy and a comedy is, of course, the ending. When we don't know how the story ends, how are we to find peace? Perhaps that's why, much to the annoyance of my wife, when I'm watching the latest thriller series, I am often caught doing a quick internet search to find out how the characters make it through. I feel safer when I can see how the confusing details of the narrative contribute to a grander story.

Here lies our problem with Paul's declaration in verse 7. When he said this, he was right in the middle of a narrative. He wasn't at a safe distance. He is no armchair theologian, but literally battling at the sharp end of hard times. There's no indication in Scripture that his thorn ever went away, or that at the time of writing, his problems were in the rearview mirror. On the contrary, he is under attack, with the weapon of choice being character assassination for his apparent weakness from this thorn. Yet he begins his reflection on this encounter with suffering and unanswered prayer by looking to the end of the bigger picture of what God is working out. When he looks, he sees a God who is "keeping me."

And Paul is not the first in Scripture to see this. Psalm 121 is a beautiful, hope-filled assertion that the Lord will keep your spiritual life: "He will not let your foot be moved; he who keeps you will not slumber. Behold, he who keeps Israel will neither slumber nor sleep" (Psalm 121:3–4 ESV)

Though we wish we had steadfast feet of faith, we know we need God's intervention as we live out our new lives in Christ. The Hebrew word for *keep* is taken from a shepherding context. Imagine a tender shepherd constructing a fence of protection to guard the sheep from a ruinous end.

Likewise, Jude and Peter set their hope for the end of the story on the keeping power of God.

> To him who is able to keep you from stumbling and to present you before his glorious presence without fault and with great joy—to the only God our Savior be glory, majesty, power and authority, through Jesus Christ our Lord, before all ages, now and forevermore! Amen. (Jude 24–25)

> Who through faith are shielded by God's power until the coming of the salvation that is ready to be revealed in the last time. (1 Peter 1:5)

It's difficult to miss the promised intent and ability of the Lord in these verses to keep his people *from* something and *to* something. The same is happening in 2 Corinthians 12:7 for Paul. As he broadens his gaze out from the pain he is facing, he is confident that it is not meant to kill him, but part of the process to keep him.

I wish my one-year-old daughter could have broadened her gaze when I took her for her first inoculations. Those two needle pricks on the same day were a vital part of her medical welfare, in order to keep her from things that could kill her. I knew it was the way things had to be, yet I'd been dreading it. I'd told my wife as much, and I didn't want to have any part of my little daughter being jabbed with a needle, but due to other commitments on my wife's calendar at the designated time, it was up to me. As I tried to hide my apprehension while heading into the treatment room, I remember little Bethany being blissfully happy in Daddy's arms, unaware of what I was carrying her to. The nurse, who had done this a thousand times before, could sense my agitation, so she gave me clear, assertive instructions. "Hold her leg tightly with your hands, and hold her gaze with your eyes." I did as I was told. Out of Bethany's line of sight, I caught her glancing away as the cruel instrument penetrated her chubby left thigh. Her gaze shifted from me to what had pierced her, and the heartbreaking scream followed a delayed intake of breath. I'm not sure who was shaking more.

But it wasn't over yet, and now she was wise to what was going on. I'll never forget the look she gave me as I began to repeat the process by gripping her right thigh. Her beautiful, innocent eyes looked into mine as if she were asking questions that were beyond her powers of speech: *Why are you doing this, Daddy? Aren't I supposed to be totally safe with you? What possible good could come of this?* When the second needle went in, she made no noise; she just looked at me with a tear rolling out of each eye. "Are you OK?" asked the nurse in a gentle and reassuring voice. After a moment's pause, I looked up and realized she was saying it not to Bethany, but to me! There were tears in my eyes too.

What I battled with that day, and what Bethany was oblivious to, were very real pathogens that could do her serious harm and even take her life. Taking her to the nurse was part of my keeping her from what could destroy her in the future. Paul saw that he needed the same kind of keeping in terms of his spiritual life.

I wonder if you'll allow this to help you glory in the scope of your redemption in Christ. Not only has he offered you life but also he is keeping you in that same spiritual life. The Christian hope is not about making struggling people slightly more comfortable but about making spiritually dead people alive to God in Christ and keeping them there. This is his grace to us. We need ongoing protection after our conversion to keep us from falling into spiritual ruin.

The difficulty for us, and the disappointment for a Corinthian church fluent in its own awesomeness, is that his keeping power doesn't always look like a pain-free life. Paul frames his struggle, his battle, his thorn, as a sign that God was dealing with him more personally than ever before. He was being kept for God, and from something ruinous.

KEEPING ME *FROM . . .*

What is it that is so ruinous for the human soul before a God of grace? The answer is conceit. Paul explains it this way: "To keep me from becoming conceited because of the surpassingly great revelations" (2 Corinthians 12:7 ESV).

"Conceit" is a word that has gone out of style in modern culture, but we know it when we see it. In hushed conversations people make comments about others being "full of themselves," and we know exactly what that means. It means being lifted up in their (and our) own eyes—lifted up in pride. It is a destructive self-sufficiency that tricks us out of our need of God. It boasts in and finds significance in our goals, desires, achievements, and worldly ambition. It hides inside each of us, seeking to pollute each of our estimated sixty thousand daily thoughts with a sense of self-interest and self-importance. Yet it is sneaky and difficult to see in ourselves because it blinds us with an inflated or excessive confidence in our own judgment and ability. Our wisdom, desires, and actions take center stage, so that the grace of God to us in Christ becomes the understudy to our performance, pretense, plans, and potential. We may not consciously want to do it, but our hearts naturally drift in the direction of conceit.

So verse 7 is really Paul's way of saying, "Let me tell you a good thing that God did in order to keep me from becoming cocky!" Do you remember, in the previous verses, that Paul talks about a level of spiritual privilege—a good gift that has come down from above? In a room full of people throwing their puny egos around, this truly is a humdinger of a party stopper. As they fall over themselves trying to outdo one another, the room goes quiet as Paul lets on to the mysterious privilege that has shaped him. Speaking in the third person, he recounts an experience of being carried up into the third heaven. He got to see things that no one but him could see, things of God's goodness and grace, with the risen Lord Jesus as his tour guide—a gift to sustain and encourage him for his ministry, to prepare his heart for the things ahead that he must do in Jesus's name (2 Corinthians 12:1–4). What an uplifting gift of grace! But though he had this good thing that came into his life, he had a bad thing in his heart. The human heart will do very strange things with good gifts in our lives. They can become an occasion for us to believe that we are more than we really are.

We can imagine the inner dialogue that could have started to percolate through Paul's mind: *I'm pretty special, aren't I? I can do this! I've been given this privilege for a reason, and that's because of me! I must be wise and strong. I can be something. I deserve to be recognized and respected.* We see how the conceit hiding in our hearts is so spiritually ruinous. Its tantalizing taste snuffs out dependent faith and replaces it with the empty promise of self. But if you are full of yourself, you cannot be full of the Lord.

Faith delights to say, "I am established and have standing by the worth of Christ." Conceit clamors to say, "I am established and have standing on my own worth and merit."

Faith delights to say, "Though weak and needy, I am freely loved by Christ." Conceit clamors to say, "I can be strong and earn love."

Faith delights to say, "My life is for the glory of God." Conceit clamors to say, "My life is for the advancement of me."

Faith delights to say, "The love of Christ is all I need." Conceit clamors to say, "I'll decide what I need."

Faith delights to say, "Eternity is coming." Conceit clamors to say, "I will seek my heaven here."

Faith delights to say, "He is going to keep me." Conceit says, "He is killing me."

Could there be any more important thing for Paul's life and ministry than to be kept from soul-poisoning, ministry-ruining, Satan-echoing conceit?

Paul's admission of this tractor beam-like pull toward subtle expressions of conceit, even after huge spiritual privilege, should make us pause in thought. Paul went to heaven and back and still couldn't be trusted to do the right thing! His honesty gives us an opportunity to agree with the Bible's tough assumption that the most-needed change, in any of our lives as followers of Jesus, is not in our situation or circumstance but within ourselves. Often our knowledge of Jesus, past spiritual growth, and general sincerity of desire to honor Jesus can fool us into thinking, *I know my heart, and I want what is right!* Yet as Craig Groeschel points out,

> It is easy to pretend that we are good at heart, but the Bible teaches us that our hearts deceive us and are desperately wicked. At its core our heart is about self, not Christ. It is about the temporary, not the eternal. It is about what is easy, not what is right. It is obsessed with what we want, not what God wants.[1]

Until we fully acknowledge the chaos within us (what the Bible calls sin), we live in what the theologian John Calvin calls unreality.[2] This may surprise us, but it is not a surprise to the God of grace. When he called us in Christ and named us as his own, he knew the process that was ahead. He knows what lurks in each human soul. He knew the intricacies of conceit in Paul's heart, and he knows the same intricacies in each of us. We may be blind to the danger, but he is not. Yet rather than be repulsed and retreat in rightful indignation at our sin, he brings remedies tailored to the specific tendencies that pour out of us in any given moment as we seek to leverage so many good things in our lives for our own selfish, God-denying purposes.

As we begin to see this keeping priority of God for his children, we get a sense of what God is doing in the details of our lives. This is what is being worked out in the process of redemption. He is *keeping* us. It's by no means the only thing that he is doing in our lives. In any given moment, his sovereign grace is working out a thousand things, of which we can only dimly discern a few from our vantage point. Yet this is a very big one. Could it be that in our experience of "I prayed but nothing changed," he is keeping us from our soul-destroying self-sufficiency?

Many have said that there are only three ways the Lord answers prayer: "Yes," "No," and "Wait." But that kind of simplicity doesn't tell the full story. The *way* that the Lord says "No" is what really matters. Is it the "No" of a harsh schoolmaster, or is it the tender words of our Savior who has already proved his eternal love for you, saying, "No, dear child; if I give you this, it will wreak havoc in your life"? Even as we hear that tender voice, we can be so wedded to our sorrow or desire that we question his goodness, generosity, and love. We might think, *If God doesn't deliver the goods, then why pray at all?* And in those thoughts we have revealed our hand—we view God merely as a tool for achieving what we want, as if he were a vending machine in whom we deposit our prayers to elevate our lot in accordance with our wisdom. We have downgraded the Sovereign Lord who saves to the level of a genie in a bottle.

What would it say of his love if he capitulated to this? He would not be keeping us. He would be killing us. Praise him that he is faithful to keep us from conceit.

KEEPING ME *TO* . . .

Are you comforted by this? Well, Lisa wasn't! Those unmet desires, the accompanying emotional pain, and the reinforced imaginings of how she wanted her life to be felt more present to her than God's loving keeping. Of course, I could see why. It's hard to see past our hearts' declarations about what we really "need" in a given moment. We get more proficient at thinking thoughts that we dwell on. They settle in with practice. As the meditations of Lisa's heart formed around "God is killing me," slowly, but surely, she'd become set in that way of thinking. Perhaps your experience is similar. Without realizing it, we can start to justify thoughts and emotions that are a flat-out denial of Christ's present love and grace.

Yet Paul, throughout this letter, speaks so warmly of the comfort he receives from the Lord. We can see Paul delighting in Christ's comfort, despite the Lord doing this difficult work of keeping him from conceit. In fact, it's more personal than that. The Lord is actively keeping him in comfort:

> Praise be to the *God and Father of our Lord Jesus Christ, the Father of compassion and the God of all comfort*, who comforts us in all our troubles, so that we can comfort those in any trouble with the comfort we ourselves receive from God. For just as we share abundantly in the sufferings of Christ, so also our comfort abounds through Christ. (2 Corinthians 1:3–5, emphasis added)

This early sentence sets the tone for the whole letter. It's the filter through which Paul saw everything. It envelops all his experiences: receiving a thorn, battling against conceit, and dealing with church leaders who heralded their own awesomeness, among others. These were his troubles, but he chose to experience them glorying in the comfort of the Lord keeping him in them.

So here's the key to experiencing the comfort of Christ: conceit and comfort can't dwell simultaneously in the same heart. They are at war, and only one can win in any moment. When conceit rules in the heart, it cuts us off from the comfort of the Lord, because we won't let the precious prizes of redemption and grace have the final word. In conceit, we must have our version of comfort. We complain that the Lord is not giving us comfort, while clinging to comfort only as we have defined it. Conceit says, "The comfort of the Lord really isn't that comforting compared to the comfort that I am looking for." And so it isn't! Our hearts fulfill their own prophecy! Conceit and comfort will battle, but only one will win.

I've experienced this as a preacher. I regularly pray that when I open God's Word with his people, he would comfort them with a gospel hope. I've found that the sermons that my congregation appreciated most have been those that have comforted *me* the most. Those were sermons I preached when I was disappointed in myself, despairing amid difficulties, and despondent about the future, while still lifting up the grace of Christ as our hope. I have sensed while preaching the comfort of God in times of trouble, and my heart has been built up in faith. A surrender to the precious promises of God brings peace, hope, and acceptance that is truly soul-sustaining, in spite of the troubles still going on all around. I've felt kept and held by the tender hands of the Savior.

But then the war begins—the war in my heart. The weapons of the Enemy are encouragements from those who heard—compliments and words of appreciation for the word that I had given. Conceit starts to rise within me, and I chew over those juicy, hellish morsels in my mind. They cater to my pretensions to self-sufficiency for whatever life brings. "You can do this!" they whisper. It is an almost visceral feeling, capturing thoughts and emotions, as I feel the center of my comfort draining from Christ to my own achievements and success. It is ugly, deceitful, and frequently successful at ensnaring me. I hold Christ's comfort at arm's length, in favor of a flimsy, conceit-drenched, fast-fading approval from others. The comfort of the Lord and conceit cannot dwell together.

I need to give permission for one to have authority over the other, but I can't do that on my own. It is the same for you. Mere intellectual consent to the theological truth that God keeps you will glance off a heart that hasn't actively surrendered those tasty morsels of self-will. I will be resentful of his care and demand my own version of what I want. Instead, I need the Spirit of God to help me see Christ again, and again, and again.

This is why verse 5 follows verses 3 and 4: "For just as we share abundantly in the sufferings of Christ, so also our comfort abounds through Christ" (2 Corinthians 1:5).

Paul holds up to the Corinthian church the One who himself was due all exaltation, and who most deserved to be lifted up, by speaking of *how* he was lifted up. The Puritans often spoke of the whole of the life of the Lord Jesus as his humiliation. One who deserved to be lifted high was lifted up to a cross in humiliation, bearing the shame of a conceit-addicted world. Christ himself describes it: "And I, when I am lifted up from the earth, will draw all people to myself" (John 12:32). What a strange dynamic—that as we see Jesus lifted up for us, denied all comfort, with his sufferings flowing into our lives to guarantee us a life we have neither earned nor deserved, we are strangely drawn *to* him and *away from* conceit. The power of the cross softens our hearts. God is keeping us *to his* comfort as we surrender conceit at the foot of the cross.

A DAILY PRAYER FOR CHRIST'S COMFORT

Jesus, you know how I am made, you know how I think, and you know how quickly the comfort I desire crowds out the true comfort you offer in yourself. Please turn this wayward heart back to you. I know my only hope is in you, but your Spirit must drive that truth deep into my soul. Thank you for the grace of keeping me. Thank you for your comfort. Thank you that you are a Man of Sorrows, well acquainted with suffering. You know my troubles; help me to know you and love you. Amen.

Chapter 3

HE GIVES

It didn't feel like a gift—this rude and unexpected intrusion that had upended the happy status quo of our lives.

Any number of overpowering circumstances could come at us in this broken world. We live on the ragged edge of a whole host of potential threats—a betrayal by a spouse, a cancer diagnosis, a financial calamity, the loss of a child, and many other tragedies can threaten us. When these threats strike—sometimes suddenly and other times like a slow train wreck rumbling toward us down the tracks—we know they are going to pierce us, hurt us, and unsettle everything. When life feels chaotic and out of control, waves of unprocessed emotion swirl around us, both mobilizing us to try to survive and flattening us with exhaustion. We feel many things—perhaps chiefly an unpalatable cocktail of fear and sorrow—when we survey the wreckage of what we held dear and wonder how to adapt to whatever has changed. We feel many things, but not that we have been given a precious gift!

Receiving a panicked call from my daughter, I raced to the park where she and my wife, Jane, had been cycling. Instinctive prayers were pouring out of my mouth and heart because it sounded bad: "Lord, please don't let this be serious. Have mercy and shelter us with your grace."

I found Jane on the ground in terrible pain. There was a crowd around her all telling me what had happened—a seeming freak accident as a dog with no leash had been chased into the road, just as the group of cyclists rode by. As they braked suddenly, Jane's front wheel caught on the gears of the bike in front, accelerating her over the handlebars, with her shoulder taking the full force of the impact with the road's raised curb. Praise the Lord, she wasn't dead. But although it happened in a fraction of a second, it took more than a year for us to understand the full extent of the damage.

Though she was just about in one piece, her shoulder was not. The following days were full of consultations with doctors and specialists. They would confidently lay out the best-case scenario that they were working for in order to rescue the shoulder and its function, with a tagged-on worst-case scenario just in case. So we prayed, thinking surely the Lord, the "Father of compassion and the God of all comfort" (2 Corinthians 1:3) would be pleased to hear and answer those prayers. But yes, you guessed it, the opposite of what we were praying for emerged every time, with yet more bad news and disappointment. Our hearts sank as one cocky specialist declared, "You couldn't have smashed this up better if you had tried." Ahead of Jane, an active woman in her thirties with six school-age kids, was a shoulder replacement, no shoulder function due to irreparable nerve damage, and a life with chronic pain.

The implications of injuries like this ripple out into every area of life, disrupting the fragile manageability of day-by-day living. Despite the medications, Jane was in constant pain and barely slept for the first several months. She was left exhausted, both physically and emotionally. Though church and family wonderfully rallied around to help, we found that hard-fought-for routines in family life became near-impossible, and our parenting and pastoring of the church were running on empty. Our life had taken an unwelcome turn for the worse.

As we entered this season and walked though it together, Jane and I had no presumption that divine favor should insulate us from life's difficulties. We knew and loved the Scriptures promising that the Lord works good in the hard things that come from his hand:

> In all this you greatly rejoice, though now for a little while you may have had to suffer grief in all kinds of trials. These have come so that the proven genuineness of your faith—of greater worth than gold, which perishes even though refined by fire—may result in praise, glory and honor when Jesus Christ is revealed. (1 Peter 1:6–7)

> Consider it pure joy, my brothers and sisters, whenever you face trials of many kinds, because you know that the testing of your faith produces perseverance. (James 1:2–3)

Yet it didn't feel like a good thing or like something we could rejoice in. Instead we were longing to have the old normal restored. I'm not alone in that, am I? Just this week I had a conversation with a grief-stricken woman, a bride-to-be, who recently, on the date she was due to be married, found herself attending the funeral of her fiancé, who had been taken by cancer. Her life had been shattered, and it seemed her prayers had come to naught.

Her words to me were full of a sorrow-filled faith that God was good, that this was from his hand, and that he was working out his purposes in love. Yet she confessed that it just didn't feel like that for her in that moment. It was hard for her to believe that this sorrow was a present gift of grace, especially after so many unanswered prayers for healing and restoration seemed to have fallen on deaf ears: "How can this be a gift? Can I have my old life back please?" She had prayed, but nothing had changed.

The author Jerry Sittser speaks with refreshing candor as he reflects on the devastation to his life that came as he lost his mother, wife, and daughter in one awful moment to a car accident.

> I can imagine what my response might have been if someone had asked me on September 26th, 1991, "Do you believe that God works all things together for good? Do you believe that suffering really develops character and leads to hope?" I would have quickly and confidently replied, "Most certainly," to both questions. But at the time, I believed those promises more as theological abstraction than real conviction. My "most certainly" did, in fact, become far less certain and confident on September 28, 1991, for I faced a mess of pain and chaos that took time—a very long time—to understand and overcome.
>
> In truth, I would have liked to have remained a spoiled child. This option, however,

> was decisively and permanently eliminated on September 27, 1991. I struggled for many years before I could see the "good" come out of the accident—any new character formed in me or in my children. I'm not even sure that I wanted such good or such character. I rather preferred the life I had lost, and I longed to return to the familiar world and relationships of the past.[1]

When tragedy strikes, when disappointment camps at your door, and when any potential good seems either impossible or a long way down the tracks, is there any hope that we can endure afflictions now, with a sense that our sufferings are a present gift? As we return to Paul's personal journey through the pains of unanswered prayer, I think we will see the beginnings of a way to battle toward that hope—a hope that we can live through unanswered prayer with a sense that suffering is a gift to us, not just at some future point, but even today as we struggle. Let's look at his words. Paul said, "I was given a thorn in my flesh, a messenger of Satan, to torment me" (2 Corinthians 12:7).

The language of a thorn is something that we can all relate to: an experience of a pain that has to be lived with—one that pierces and won't leave. A brief review of Paul's life, even just his honesty in this letter to the Corinthian church, reveals that hardships, sufferings, and afflictions were common occurrences in his life and ministry. In chapter 11 he details a truly terrifying catalog of experiences that would bring even the most determined overcomer to despair:

> I have worked much harder, been in prison more frequently, been flogged more severely, and been exposed to death again and again. Five times I received from the Jews the forty lashes minus one. Three times I was beaten with rods, once I was pelted with stones, three times I was shipwrecked, I spent a night and a day in the open sea, I have been constantly on the move. I have been in danger from rivers, in danger from bandits, in danger from my fellow Jews, in danger from Gentiles; in danger in the city, in danger in the country, in danger at sea; and in danger from false believers. I have labored and toiled and have often gone without sleep; I have known hunger and thirst and have often gone without food; I have been cold and naked. (2 Corinthians 11:23–27)

Even after all that, he has singled out this particular thorn. Bible scholars have speculated as to its nature, but we must assume that Paul intentionally does not spell it out. It's not what it is that is important, but what it does: "to torment me," or "to buffet me." So at some point in his life, no doubt soon after the great revelations of heaven that were given him to build him up (2 Corinthians 12:1–6), something else was given him that had become a trying, constant companion—a demonic henchman to knock him off his stride, buffet him, rough him up, and kick him when he's down. The word is close to the idea of "to hit with a clenched fist." Think of daily body blows that knock the physical, spiritual, and emotional wind out of him.

Though he had visited heaven, hell was dragging along after him every day. We must not miss the fact, in this chapter of Scripture, that of the two experiences that Paul received—a vision of heaven and a walk in hell—it is the latter that he wants to speak of more to his beloved brothers in Christ in Corinth.

GIVEN PERSONALLY

Paul recognizes that this thorn was given to him personally: "there was given me." He seems to be saying something like this: "My sufferings were given by God; therefore, God is in my troubles, and therefore I can see my troubles as a gift." We struggle to conceive of a God that would intentionally and deliberately bring sorrow or powerlessness into the lives of his loved ones. We can be helped and comforted, perhaps, that "he does not willingly bring affliction or grief to anyone" (Lamentations 3:33). But then there is the story of Job. If he is sovereign, then all the details of timing, down to the split-second orchestration of a road-traffic accident, or the millimeter precision of the cutting of nerve endings in an operation, are ultimately the responsibility of the living God. To put it brutally, if Paul is in pain, it is because God wants him there. It seems that God personally gives pain to those he loves.

This would be a pretty bleak picture if taken in isolation from the other thing that Paul has told us that the believers had been given: "his grace given you in Christ Jesus" (1 Corinthians 1:4). Here Paul is using a catchall phrase that summarizes the full sweep of the redemption that believers have and will have in Christ—redemption that spans from being loved and known in election from before the beginning of time, through Christ coming to redeem and forgive at the cost of his precious blood, to being caught up in future glory in Jesus Christ when the fulfillment of the age is upon us. It is precisely in the presence of painful, humbling thorns that we have this glorious redemption worked out in us.

But make no mistake: the thorns that you are given are just as personally given by the Lord (who knows you and loves you) as his precious gift of gracious redemption in Christ. Paul was precious in the Lord's sight and known to him. So are you. As Joe Thorn (no pun intended) celebrates,

> He knows what you really need, not just what you ask for. He knows what will break you and what will help you. He knows what you can handle and what is too much. So when you seek God's power, provision, or intervention, you do not have to worry about his response. He will not get it wrong. He knows you and knows exactly how to answer you.[2]

So often, our instinctive reaction to our seemingly senseless sufferings and to our prayers that seem to return without the change we want is to ask, "Why?" There might be some consolation in being able to put the details together in some sort of flowchart that might help us understand what's happening. Yet few of us, as we are facing affliction, have the luxury of an angel appearing by our side to give us that level of detail. That is for the Lord to know, and that is for him alone. We are simply asked to trust our heavenly Father—that the thorn that flattens you is a vital and necessary part of the broader grace of Christ working out in you and through you to a world that he is redeeming. We are asked to trust that particular and personal pain is given personally for a particular design.

When speaking of his own battle with cancer, pastor John Piper provocatively warns other believers that they will waste their cancer if they do not believe it is given to them by God.

> It will not do to say that God only uses our cancer but does not design it. . . . What God permits, he permits for a reason. And that reason is his design. If God sees molecular developments becoming cancer, he can stop it or not. If he does not, he has a purpose. Since he is infinitely wise, it is right to call this purpose a design. . . . If you don't believe that your cancer is designed for you by God, you will waste it.[3]

And is that not what we long for—to know that every detail of our often mundane and ordinary existences adds up to something that will echo to the glory of Christ in eternity? If a pain has come your way, you can be sure that not only has the Lord signed off on it but also that it is a vital part of his redemption plan for the whole world. Paul's pain was. It was given personally. No wonder that the saints down the ages have joined with Thomas A. Kempis in his prayer, "O Lord, you know what is best for me. Give me whatever you will, how much you will and when you will."[4]

GIVEN INTENTIONALLY

Echoing many themes in the book of Job, Paul sees two intentions at play in his sufferings. Seeing these will help us better grasp why we find it so hard to see our sorrows and unanswered prayers as gifts to us. In the same thorn, Paul sees the *immediate* cause, which is Satan's intention to hurt and destroy by lying about the goodness and personal care of God, and the *ultimate* cause—God using Satan's schemes to achieve the opposite of Satan's plans.

On first reading, what Paul is saying is shocking: "A messenger of Satan was given me." What kind of God allows Satan to beat up on his precious children? An emissary of our adversary was sent by God—given by God—to bring pain and weakness into Paul's life. "God permitted the devil to harass me," says the apostle.

This is where the book of Job is so helpful. You see, the book starts with Satan sniffing around the world, trying to find ways to ruin God's plan to bring grace and mercy to a lost humanity. We see an encounter in heaven where the Lord draws attention to Job. "Then the Lord said to Satan, 'Have you considered my servant Job? There is no one on earth like him; he is blameless and upright, a man who fears God and shuns evil'" (Job 1:8). And then Satan comes along with his blasphemous lies, and says, "Does Job fear God for nothing?" (Job 1:9).

This is the blasphemy. In the presence of God, the Enemy is saying, "I get why Job does that. It's not because you are wholly good. It's not because you are worthy, or glorious, or because you have loved him with an endless love. It's not because you are the hope of the humanity that you have made. People aren't ultimately satisfied in you, God. Job loves you because you give the goodies! You reshape his life in the way that he likes, and the second that that's taken away, he will walk out." This actually becomes the question of the book: Does Job fear God for no reason?

But this isn't just the question of Job, is it? It's often the question that is hanging over us when our lives don't go the way we want and when God doesn't answer our prayers in the way we think he should. It was playing out in Corinth, too, as the church there seemed deeply dissatisfied with their struggles in life. It's one of the things that Paul is trying to impress upon the Corinthian church: God in himself, and his saving love in Christ, are gloriousness in themselves (2 Corinthians 2–3). We love God for God, not for the goodies he gives us.

Satan wants to discredit the greatness, goodness, and grace of God in Christ. He wants to perpetuate the lie of the garden of Eden; that is, he wants to say (in essence), "God doesn't love you. You can live better without him." And Paul sees in this thorn the Enemy's attempt to drag him away from Christ, to discredit Paul in the eyes of other believers, and to destroy him as a minister of the gospel.

Now, please understand that the devil is not an equal of God. He is not omniscient, he is not omnipresent, and he is certainly not omnipotent. He doesn't have the power. He has to get permission. But if he needs to get permission, what does that also mean for us? It means that if that permission is withdrawn, he cannot do any more. We need to know that the devil is under God's power—just as all of creation is. Let me tell you that no demon can do what God does not permit. So why does he permit this? Why does God allow this messenger to have any rope to hang Paul with? What is the Lord's intention?

It seems that the Lord is giving Satan just enough rope, in both Job's life and Paul's, to hang himself. Satan will have enough permission, and can only bring enough hurt, to destroy his own intention to discredit God in the life of Job and Paul. And this is how it works in us too. The Lord only permits thorns to come to the degree that defeats Satan's wider purpose to rob God's people of life.

The proof of that is sitting in your hand right now! No doubt you are reading this book in faith and hope that you can push past what you are going through to find more of the God who feels obscured by your pain. God's people, when suffering, come to battle with sorrow, loss, self-pity, grumbling, and questioning (much like Job). We pray for things to change or for a personal explanation. As God allows some of his gifts of common grace to be taken away, we fight to say with Job, "The Lord gave and the Lord has taken away; may the name of the Lord be praised" (Job 1:21).

As God draws near to us, we start to see what Paul says here—that God and his grace in Christ to us are bigger than we first realized. We cling to him. Is that not what is behind you reading this book? That you might see him? You are, right now, fulfilling one of his gracious intentions in allowing a messenger of Satan. He intends to pull you closer to himself, the One who is your ultimate source of life.

Only the gift of a thorn can do that. There is only one way to learn to really love God alone. And it's not when he is giving you all the things you pray for but when you are suffering and only have him left. Every day of difficulty is a gift in this sense. You have an opportunity to love God, but not for the things you love that he gives you because they are being removed by Satan's devices and God's permission. You get to love God not for the goodies he gives but for the glory that is within himself. So the very thorn that was sent with evil intent to destroy you and discredit your heavenly Father actually drives you closer into your hope in his rescuing and redeeming grace.

The very experiences that would seem to drive you furthest from God are the same experiences that bring you into the closest fellowship with the Savior. Without an awareness of this, I don't know how you will cope when believers in trouble come to share their story with you. Without this hope, all you will have to offer them is commiseration. Yet, even if they seem far from this hope, you know that the Lord is working something out in them. Their dark night of the soul will give way to joy.

Satan is very good at making us feel like the thorns in our lives are anything but gifts. But when we dare to see that the Lord has given them intentionally, we begin to dare to put off doubt and rejoice that he is winning not just *over* the thorn but *through* the thorn. It is only when Satan steals that which we thought to be life that we find true life. That is God's intentional gift to you today in your thorn. Do you feel it yet?

GIVEN ILLUSTRATIVELY

Paul chooses the language and images in this passage carefully. For anyone familiar with the cross of Christ, they are too vivid to miss: a thorn, which is better understood as a spike or a nail that pierces through flesh; the torment or buffeting—the blows with a closed fist that knock their victim around; the whispers of Satan, to tempt us away from the way of suffering, which is the way of fulfilling the Lord's purpose. Christ submitted himself to all these things for our salvation.

Paul wants us to map our suffering onto the sufferings of Jesus on the cross, out of which came glory and life for all his people. These unwanted and painful experiences, though evil in and of themselves, are in Paul's life an echo or illustration of a greater thorn and buffeting, which would give way to a greater glory—the restoration of all things. They are an illustration of nothing less than the cross of Christ, the place of our redemption and means of his renewing of the world. He is living a cross-shaped life. God's way is that suffering will give way to glory. And this is not the first time Paul has understood his sufferings through this lens.

> For just as we share abundantly in the sufferings of Christ, so also our comfort abounds through Christ. (2 Corinthians 1:5)

> We always carry around in our body the death of Jesus, so that the life of Jesus may also be revealed in our body. For we who are alive are always being given over to death for Jesus' sake, so that his life may also be revealed in our mortal body. (2 Corinthians 4:10–11)

This is why Paul was so unpopular in this self-sufficient church in Corinth. It is hard to see how sufferings and loss in our life could flow over into comfort. It's harder still to see how a death is the route to life.

When we are caught up in our disappointment at the pain that has interrupted our ordered lives, it is nearly impossible to feel that becoming like Jesus in his death could be a gift. It's why I get so panicked when the Lord complicates my life with painful intrusions or takes away much-loved grace gifts. Its why I don't feel that thorns are a gift. For me to see that, it would require me to see all the suffering in my life through the lens of what my Savior was doing when he endured the cross. I would have to believe that glory reveals itself in weakness, not strength. Or as Mike Emlet bravely points out to people (like my wife) who are facing a life of pain, "Your pain today is actually part of the engine that drives forward redemptive history. It drives forward, pushing back the curse. Suffering and glory: that's the currency of the kingdom."[5]

Since I grew up as a wrestling fan, you can imagine my surprise when, while scrolling through new Christian biographies, I came upon the story of one of my childhood fascinations, Lex Luger, also known as "The Total Package" and "The Narcissist." He gained worldwide fame as a pro wrestling champion. He stood six feet, four inches tall, weighed 265 pounds, and had a thirty-two-inch waist. His muscles were like polished steel, and his perfectly sculpted body added to the wrestling mania that had gripped the world. He marketed himself as the picture of human strength and self-sufficiency. Given what I knew about the man, I had to read it. The first part of the story outlined his meteoric rise and life of fame and excess. But then there was the descent into loss, addiction, jail time, and ultimately physical disability. He is now riddled with orthopedic problems and looks the very opposite of his early-life persona. Yet, through hearing the gospel, he was brought to Christ and now has a prominent outreach ministry.

As I came to the close of the book, delighting in God's grace to this former idol of mine, I found myself wondering what could have been if the Lord had saved this man when he had been at the height of his strength and celebrity. He looked so impressive then, but now he looks pretty unimpressive. He looked like an overcomer and would have garnered so much worldly attention. Now he is a picture of all the suffering the world wishes to avoid. Wouldn't he have been a better ambassador for Jesus twenty years earlier, before he had the chance to flush all his worldly capital down the toilet?

Yet those ponderings have merely revealed just how Corinthian I am. Like the Corinthians, I can't see how a place characterized by suffering and brokenness is where God does his best work and overcomes the world. I can't see how embracing suffering puts me in solidarity with Jesus and manifests him to the world. I don't mind receiving new life from Jesus, but becoming like him in his death feels like it's too much right now. I don't want to be an illustration of Jesus.

You are reading this book because a thorn has pierced you, and you have prayed for a change that hasn't come. That you have been given this does not minimize your pain, nor does it mean that your pain is not without heart-wrenching sorrow. But your pain is dignified and sanctified for the sake of Jesus's glory. This is his gift to you.

When through the deep waters I call thee to go,
The rivers of sorrow shall not overflow,

For I will be with thee, thy troubles to bless,
And sanctify to you your deepest distress.[6]

You have a love gift from him. You have been given the honor of becoming like him in his death—bearing the worst that the world can throw at you, while also imaging and illustrating his overcoming of sin, Satan, and suffering at the cross.

When Paul uses the phrase "there was given me," it doesn't carry the idea of casually sliding something your way for you to take or leave as you choose. Rather, it is something that has been committed to you in love, granted that you may live it to the full, and entrusted with a sacred trust. You will need his grace to receive it as such, and his strength to live it out.

Paul does not model for us a passive acceptance of his "fate." Rather, he shows us the way forward in how he goes to God and tells him all his troubles—and how God speaks to him in his trouble. Ask now. Speak to him, for he hears, as we will discover more fully in the next chapter.

Martha Snell Nicholson was familiar with thorns. Gifted and capable in poetry and communication, she battled four incurable diseases over several decades of her life. Here is how she came to describe this gift:

The Thorn

I stood a mendicant [beggar] of God before His
royal throne
And begged him for one priceless gift, which I
could call my own.

I took the gift from out His hand, but as I
would depart
I cried, "But Lord, this is a thorn, and it has
pierced my heart.
This is a strange, a hurtful gift, which Thou
hast given me."
He said, "My child, I give good gifts and gave
My best to thee."
I took it home, and though, at first, the cruel
thorn hurt sore,
As long years passed, I learned, at last, to love it
more and more.
I learned He never gives a thorn without this
added grace,
He takes the thorn to pin aside the veil which
hides His face.[7]

A DAILY PRAYER FOR RECEIVING ALL OF CHRIST'S GIFTS

Loving Father, you are good. Help me to trust you as you give and as you take away. I pray that the thorns that hurt so much will turn out to help me to love you more. Please don't let me waste what I have been given, but bless my troubles and hurts so that through them, I know and show Jesus more.

Chapter 4

HE HEARS

Scott had come a long way over the last few years as he fought his way back from a debilitating addiction that had cost him a marriage, a job, and so much of his dignity. Yet, this gentle and caring man lived with the fear that his destructive tendencies to medicate his emotion with alcohol were never far away from him. He loathed the self-pity and shame that accompanied his binges, but he knew that they didn't leave him in a wretched enough condition to keep him from bingeing again. He knew he needed divine help to take them away, so he prayed.

Having not seen or heard from him in a few weeks, I was worried. By chance I saw him waiting by a bus stop in our neighborhood, so I pulled over, hoping he would be willing to talk. His appearance confirmed my suspicions that he had given himself over to the addiction once again. My heart went out to him. He found it difficult to look at me, so I tried a smile and warm handshake to put him at ease. And then out it came—a lament of psalm-like categories and proportions—as the realities of life battled with his confused faith in the God of the Bible.

"People always say that God has a plan for your life. So what happened to the plan for my life? Is this it? How can that be? I'm failing, and it's getting worse. I'm trying so hard, but it's one thing after another. Does God really hear me?"

What did you hear most loudly from that heartfelt outburst? Read it again and pick out the key themes. And then try something even more challenging: ask yourself not just *what* you heard but *how* you heard it.

I heard a jumbled-up and confused stream of pain, confusion about God's ways, desperate desires for struggles to be taken away, complaints, subtle anger over how hard it is, and fears that it will always be so hard. But above all else, the haunting conclusion, as measured by his circumstances, was that God did not care enough to hear his pleading for help. And when being heard is the currency of connection and relationship, my friend was feeling abandoned and alone with his struggle. Do you have your own bleak struggle with that experience?

But how did you hear his lament? Perhaps you heard his backstory, and although you were trying to be compassionate, you felt that he has only himself to blame, so he really has no right to complain. Or perhaps you found yourself right back in the dark moments of your deepest despair, sharing his feelings, desperate for Someone to hear you, but unsure if anyone cares enough to listen. Perhaps you found yourself sharing in his anger that God hasn't done more or changed more and that God owes an explanation for the difficulty and pain of our lives. Perhaps you are unmoved, resigned to live with a stoic acceptance that pain and suffering will always assail our storm-tossed lives; hence, you think it is best to keep quiet and carry on. Perhaps you hear his cry a different way. But be sure of this: how you hear my friend's pleading to be heard will tell me something about how you think God hears the cries of his people. Does God hear you? How can you be sure? And how does God hear you? What is his posture to you as you tell him your need?

Sadly, when we have prayed and nothing has changed, we try to get those answers from our own contorted reading of the circumstances we are experiencing. We can judge God through the lens of our difficulties and make huge conclusions about who he is, what he is doing, what he is like, and whether he cares. And the feeling of being abandoned only further distorts our conclusions.

And that is why, like so many others, my friend Scott could be found at a bus stop. He had removed himself from the community of faith and stopped doing business with God. He had backed away. On one level, it is a natural step to take when you feel abandoned and unheard; yet, as Mark Vroegop points out in his deeply moving book on lament, *Dark Clouds, Deep Mercy*, "Giving God the silent treatment is the ultimate expression of unbelief. Despair lives under the hopeless resignation that God does not care, he does not hear, and nothing is going to change."[1]

You might be giving our heavenly Father the silent treatment right now. There are pains, struggles, confusion, and complaint that you have brought to everybody but him. As a lady recently said to me, "God and I are not on speaking terms." And even if you are warmed by his invite to "pour out your hearts to him" (Psalm 62:8), you may find guilt that comes from avoiding your Father to be a temptation for you to stay away longer because you fear that you will not receive a warm welcome.

The apostle Paul has his own story of praying during a protracted period of pain. He speaks to the Corinthian church of facing the terrible possibility that the Lord might not pull the thorn out: "Three times I pleaded with the Lord to take it away from me" (2 Corinthians 12:8).

His struggle was not sanitized or triumphalistic but gritty and real. He offers back to us again the hope that in vulnerable, confused, and weak-seeming prayer, we are connected to the promises of redemption in Christ and a Father who hears the pleading of his children. We, far from being abandoned, are offered a warm welcome that he has personally provided at his own expense.

HE HEARS OUR PLEAS TO DRAW US NEAR

On first reading, Paul's account of pleading with the Lord is not something that I would have thought he wanted to be shouting about. It would have sounded far from impressive to the Corinthians who were so impressed with spiritual strength and worldly shows of power. Surely, being heard by the Lord is worthless to anyone unless it delivers the provision that we are looking for. Paul's story seems to echo the fears of so many—that prayer is a colossal waste of time.

We understand that this thorn came to him soon after he had the grand revelation, when he had seen something of the heavenlies, fourteen years prior to writing this letter. Yet he was quickly moved from the mountaintop of awesome to the valley of awful. This thorn—this affliction—came into his life, and through that season, on multiple occasions (at least three) he had approached

God with empty hands and an aching heart to present his desperate petition. He models to us that whatever you are facing, you can talk to God about it. He wants you to bring your need before his throne of grace.

So, with genuine confidence in the Lord, Paul had, like Job and the psalmists before him, persistently turned his pain and confusion toward heaven in the hopes of gaining the relief he so craved. Remember, we are told by the Lord Jesus himself that we should "always pray and not give up" (Luke 18:1).

But what if over a prolonged period of time, you have come to God, and it seems as if there's silence? You've pressed in, and you've run to the Lord. You've complained, and you've been tired with the groaning of doing it, and you've said, "I'm not going to let God give me 'no' for an answer. This is too important. This is too big."

Yet no matter how ardently you have prayed, the marriage still breaks up, the child still remains wayward, the neighbors still reject Jesus, the store still closes down, the church still splits, or the recovering alcoholic still slips, even though you have prayed persistently. What happens after that? More disappointment! This is not a good advertisement for prayer in the midst of adversity.

But you are in good company. Paul and countless others have prayed for something that mattered dearly to them, for years and for seasons. They prayed again and again, only to end with not getting the answer they begged God for. This is confusing. This is mysterious. Does this mean the Lord does not hear? And while there is comfort in knowing that you are not the only one who faces such disappointments, it is certainly not comforting enough to carry you through trials with joy and hope.

To unravel this mystery, let's reconsider why Paul lets us in on this experience of unanswered prayer. Though he desperately desired the outcome for which he pleaded, perhaps there was something else of supreme comfort and value that was available to him completely apart from getting the answer that he wanted.

C. S. Lewis addresses this pressing issue in his book *The Magician's Nephew*, part of the Chronicles of Narnia. He introduces us to the pains of a boy named Digory. Swept up in the Narnia adventures, he lives with terrible worry about his mother's health, for she is dying. He knows that the lion Aslan can heal his mother—an obvious solution to this terribly pressing need. So, with great nervousness, he pleads for Aslan to give him the fruit that will heal his mother.

He wants to be heard so he can get what he so desperately needs. Yet at that time, Aslan appears to ignore him. "He had been desperately hoping that the lion would say 'yes'; he had been horribly afraid it might say 'no.' But he was taken aback when it did neither."[2]

As we hear Digory's thoughts, we can sense the danger of seeing Aslan as an "it," as little more than an answer to our prayers. When our need is great and our prescribed solution is our only goal, we can lose sight of the greater comfort that comes to us from the One who is with us and hearing us. Digory does what we all need to do—he dares to try one more time.

> He thought of his mother, and he thought of the great hopes he had, and how they were all dying away, and a lump came to his throat and tears in his eyes, and he blurted out:

> "But please, please won't you—can't you give me something that will cure Mother?" Up till then he had been looking at the Lion's great feet, and he looked up at its face. What he saw surprised him as much as anything in his whole life. For the tawny face was bent down near his own, and (wonder of wonders) great, shining tears stood in the Lion's eyes. They were such big, bright tears compared with Digory's own that, for a moment, he felt as if the Lion must be sorrier about his mother than he was himself.[3]

Digory had prayed, and nothing had changed. Or had it? Yes, the outward circumstances had remained unchanged, but his pleas had drawn him closer to the One who was with him. And the wonder that he saw, as he lifted his eyes away from *what* he was asking and toward *whom* he was asking, did not disappoint. This meant that everything had changed.

As Pete Grieg says,

> When we approach him again and again with some deep need—perhaps for healing, or to find a partner, or for a friend who's turned his or her back on Jesus—his eyes are not angry, bored, or cold, assessing the merits of our request and the technique of our prayer. Whenever we come to God with an open wound of longing, we come to Abba, Father who loves us deeply.[4]

This is how God hears each and every one of his beloved children in Christ. He is not too busy, inaccessible, or indifferent. Mercy and grace are the only things he knows how to do. Blinded by our pain, desire, and doubt, our repeated pleas force us to look up. And when we do we see One who absorbs our countless accusations and entertains our complaints, not because he has to but because he wants us to draw near to him as needy children to their caring Father.

Will you be a Paul or a Digory? Will you go again? You are not discarded in your painful prayers but heard. But this time, as you go to him, try shifting the weight of how you come: "Cast all your anxiety on him because he cares for you" (1 Peter 5:7).

When I think of my own journey with unanswered prayer, I have to admit to having prayers that are heavily weighted toward the first half of the verse ("all my anxieties") and less weighted toward the second half ("for he cares for you"). But the first half of the verse is more doable when I spend more time in the second half. As you direct your disappointment, confusion, and pain toward heaven, things will be trending upward—not because you get the change that you desire but because he hears you and draws near to you so you will draw near to him.

WHO IS THE LORD WHO HEARS?

But there is more to be said about who it is that Paul has pleaded with. He writes, "Three times I pleaded with the *Lord* to take it away from me" (2 Corinthians 12:8).

In prayer we connect some, and only some, of our human need to the promises of God. But what we often miss is that in any moment, we need so many things that are beyond what we can see and know. Protection, change, courage, or maybe provision—we rarely see it all.

We do not have either the capacity or the vantage point. But when we are praying to the Lord, it offers us a chance to let God be God. What we pray about is secondary to who we think we are praying to. Paul prayed with a sense of his real need, but he also prayed with a willingness to surrender the lordship of his life to One who is greater than him.

I remember speaking to a young person just a few weeks ago, talking about her situation and the aching in her heart that she wanted to be taken away from her. To her, it felt like the future she had been aspiring to had been slipping away—moment by moment—and no matter what she did, she couldn't make it right. I asked her where she had found comfort, and she said, "To be honest, it's really difficult to find that. I've been trying. I've been trying to seek God." I asked what was hardest about that, and the answer was, "It's just such a little thing for God! I'm asking for this little thing. It's so easy for him. It doesn't even seem to register on the importance levels of what's going on globally at the moment. Couldn't he just—just give me that?"

Like most of us, she was so caught up with her genuine concerns, and so overrun by her disappointment and pain, that she couldn't clearly see the truth that the Lord sees everything clearly, knows how to sort us out, and has the power to carry us in the right direction. He isn't swayed by our felt needs; he sees our deepest needs and has a good plan to meet them. We find freedom in the midst of our thorny seasons as we learn he is not the source of supply for all we want or a vending machine who coughs up what we want because we have decided that he should. He is the Lord over all and our heavenly Father, who is watching and keeping in the best and truest sense. Praying to our heavenly Father moves us from what we are asking for to whom it is we are asking. As we pour out our hearts to the Lord, we move from what we want to what he wants us to have. This happens uniquely when unanswered prayer forces us to contend with the God to whom we are praying. Unanswered prayer causes us to look deeper than what we want, need, or wish for and learn of him to whom we pray.

My pleadings through difficult times and thorny seasons have yielded surprising and unexpected blessings as they force me to move out from the vantage point of my pain and troubles and to press through to the Lord of heaven and earth. Unanswered prayer puts us on a journey of discovery as we have to walk down the dark corridor of disappointment to the beautiful room of God's sovereign, tender care for every one of our needs. Timothy Keller explains that journey of discovery like this:

> You may be filled with self-pity and with justified resentment and anger. Then you sit down to pray, and the reorientation that comes before God's face reveals the pettiness of your feelings and what feels so important to you. All your self-justifying excuses fall to the ground in pieces. Or you may feel anxiety, and as you are in prayer, you begin to wonder what you were worried about. You laugh at yourself and thank God for who he is and what he has done. It can be dramatic. It is the bracing clarity of a new perspective in the presence of God, and eventually, this can be the normal experience.[5]

HE HEARS THROUGH JESUS

Let's go back to my friend Scott. His struggle was not just "Will I be heard?" but "Can I be heard?" As I listened to him it was apparent that there was a deeper battle going on inside. His awareness of that battle only emerged through his painful experience with seemingly unanswered prayer. He came face-to-face with the undeniable reality that his sin left him with no claim on the throne of God. Scott is not alone. It would be difficult to read Paul's first letter to Timothy without being caught up in the apostle's amazement that someone like him ("chief of sinners") should have the ear of the living God (1 Timothy 1:15).

Michael Horton puts it this way:

> "God is in charge" and "God is good" do have their proper place in answering a crisis, but by themselves, apart from someone to mediate between the God of blinding glory and a miserable sinner, these assurances merely pour salt on the wound.[6]

No wonder Scott doubted that the Lord would hear him or even wanted to. Perhaps you, too, fear that heaven is closed to you because of your sin, that God has turned away, and you have no right to be heard. You carry with you the haunting feeling that heaven's throne of grace is bolted shut to the likes of you.

Or the opposite could be true. You feel your hardship so intensely and see your sin so lightly that you cannot fathom why the Lord doesn't jump at your command. You may use phrases like, "I should not be going through this," or you might be nurturing subtle anger and bitterness toward God because he is not giving you what you think you deserve.

This was Scott's greatest fear: "I have no grounds in myself to be heard. How can I know that God will hear me and wants to hear me?"

How does Paul know the Lord hears his plea? How can Scott (and you) know? The Lord must hear our plea because of what Paul alludes to: "Three times I pleaded with the Lord to take it away from me" (2 Corinthians 12:8). Paul is, on purpose, taking us to one of the darkest moments in all of Scripture—to the garden of Gethsemane. It's here that we find the ultimate expression of "I prayed and nothing changed" (Matthew 26:36–39). If you are familiar with unanswered prayer (and who isn't?), know that Jesus is infinitely more so. And though you may have no right of access on your own—in your own name—Jesus certainly did.

We see Jesus, at his hour of most dire need, voluntarily entering into the realm of unanswered prayer. His soul is overwhelmed to the point of death; his friends are sleeping; he is more lonely than he has ever been, trembling in a state of intense vulnerability. Three times, Jesus prays, "Take this away" (Mark 14:35). But nothing changes. Surely, Paul has this scene in mind when he references his own pleading with God to take away his thorn.

Often when we face our own Gethsemane (our place of pressing and unanswered prayer), we fail to relinquish control. But Jesus is not like us. In perfect obedience to his Father, Jesus gives way, praying, "not my will but yours be done" (Luke 22:42). Accepting that the cross is at hand, he yields to its certainty.

There are many things we could say about this scene, but Paul alludes to this as a person whose life is the fruit of Jesus's unanswered prayer. Christ was denied his hearing so that we could be guaranteed a hearing before the God of the universe through Christ's death and resurrection. Paul knows he is heard precisely because Christ was unheard.

That's why we pray in and through the name of Jesus. This is not a secret password or a slogan that we tag on to our prayers, but Jesus does tell us to "ask in my name" (John 14:14, 15:16). To come in the name of Jesus is to have all that we truly need. It is to pray consciously knowing that God knows more about the terror of unanswered prayer than you do, and has stepped in, in the person of Jesus, to remedy this. The grounds of our confidence that he hears us are not our method, the level of our misery, our worth, and our sincerity, but his. Jesus is alive, seated at the right hand of the Father, ever living to intercede for us—his people (Hebrews 4:14).

We may not know just how our circumstances will play out or the intricacies of the design in our struggles, but we do know that our "redeemer lives, and that in the end he will stand on the earth" (Job 19:25). So if you are calling on this Lord in the name of Jesus, you get royal access to the throne of grace. Further, he bids you to come and be heard. You are heard in Jesus's name. And this Jesus will fill your life, mind, and heart with his life-giving words to you. More on that in the next chapter.

A DAILY PRAYER IN JESUS'S NAME

Thank you that, through Jesus, I have confidence that you hear me. Forgive me for times when I think that that is a small thing. Thank you that my pleading matters to you. Forgive me for times when I have given you the silent treatment. Help me to trust that when I turn my struggles toward you, I will see something more of you that brings me hope. Help me to see that you are my gracious Lord who is drawing me near, especially at times when I'm not seeming to get what I have asked for. Amen.

Chapter 5

HE SPEAKS

As I welcomed Paul and Fiona into my office, their body language told the story of the words shared between them on the car journey to see me. With eyes barely able to look at each other, arms folded in defensive positions, and faces like thunder, they chose to sit as far apart from each other as possible. My Bible was already open, and I was ready to share some word of comfort and encouragement about the love of Christ and the hope of change. But I paused because it was obvious that other words were loudly ruling in that moment, laying a claim to their hearts and shaping every detail of how they responded to their difficulties. Words can do that because the words we hear and tell ourselves inevitably control our worlds.

I fired up a silent prayer: "You are God here; you know what they need to hear. Speak, Lord, with that voice that raises the dead!" They needed a voice that would speak a better word than the words that were rattling around in their heads and claiming authority over them and their lives.

I took a deep breath, picked up my Bible, read a verse from God's Word, and began to talk about the love of Christ for them. Unable or unwilling to lower the volume on the other words so that she could hear the only voice that calms the storm and creates something new out of brokenness, Fiona stood bolt upright and proceeded to dash out the door, mumbling, "I'm sorry, but I can't listen to this right now!" As Paul sat rolling his eyes (equally as unaffected by God's word as Fiona was), I was left with a sense that words had indeed controlled their worlds, but they were not the words of the Lord. Those life-giving words had not even been allowed a hearing.

Though Paul and Fiona's reaction was stark, it is far from uncommon. For me at least, when I am facing difficulty and have prayed and nothing has changed, my internal conversation seems to go on overdrive.

- I replay moments and try to give them meaning.
- I dwell on what is lost or may never come to pass.
- I look to what is ahead and try to talk myself into facing it.
- I imagine the criticism of others and try to construct a defense.

In the midst of my confusion and the accompanying emotional mess, I tend to hold at a distance the only thing that has created something out of nothing and redeemed what is most broken—that is, the Word of Christ.

Perhaps you know that temptation as you face the difficulties that have prompted you to pray for a change. The voices of your own self-talk, the words of the culture, and the words of people around you have controlled your world, and without realizing it, you have concluded with a shrug of the shoulders that God's words have no relevance and can wait until the end of the crisis or simply won't help. You did not want to find yourself here, but the words of Christ that once sang into your soul, filling you with hope and wisdom, have been drowned out by the volume of distorted voices. You wonder if he even wants to speak to you in your trouble.

DISTORTED VOICES AND CONTROLLING WORDS

Because I am a pastor and counselor, it may surprise you to hear that my first job is not to speak but to listen. I do this not only because I care what you are going through and not primarily to help you get something off your chest, but also so I can help you think through the distorted voices and controlling words that are rattling around inside of you, shaping your outlook during a thorny season. When we let those words control our world, we leave no room to listen to the Lord. What are some of those distorted voices that we listen to? Here's a list to get you started.

The words of others

Whatever the personal hardship that was the apostle Paul's thorn in the flesh, it was made worse by the words of others. The 'super' apostles rubbed their hands with glee as they used Paul's struggles to denounce him as inferior, attack him personally, and trash his reputation. Enemies and friends alike would put their spin on what his struggles meant for his life, ministry, and worth. And though the apostle Paul was made of strong stuff, he was not left unaffected by what was said about him. With their words, they were trying to win him to a less Christ-centered vision for his life and ministry that looked more impressive, comfortable, and satisfying from a worldly point of view. It would have been so easy for him to be lured by those voices and captured by those priorities. It is even harder when these kinds of words are said by someone whom you care about, and who is supposed to care for you.

Paul and Fiona knew something of that—mutual criticism, accusation, demands, and threats had gotten into their heads, shaped their view of each other, and exhausted their emotions. The words of others can control our worlds, leaving little room for the Lord to be heard. Is that happening to you right now?

The words of culture

We may consider the apostle Paul a spiritual giant, but by the measure of the city of Corinth, he was a novelty at best, and at worst to be despised. Much like today, the culture screamed that to find life, you must be outwardly impressive, beautiful, strong, sensual, and important. The city had a loud vision for the best life, against which it was hard not to measure yourself. That same messaging was alive and well in the local church gatherings, wooing the believers to its ideals and stirring fear of condemnation for anyone who fell short.

Paul and Fiona knew something of that—as we talked, it was plain that powerful cultural expectations about what their marriage and life together should be like were mixed in with the many Christian values they shared. Barely aware of this influence, they had drifted into accepting these voices as truth. Then things started to fall apart. Not able to deliver the designer life demanded by the cultural voices around them, they felt worthless and hopeless. They had prayed for change, but mainly to help them live up to a worldly vision for their lives. Would they be willing to hear a more gracious word for the moment they were in? The words of the culture can control our worlds, leaving little room for the Lord to be heard. What cultural voices have you given too much permission to, leaving your sense of self crushed and a nagging sense that your life is inevitably heading in the wrong direction? Those things will play loudly on repeat if we don't see them for what they are.

The words of Satan

As sure as night follows day, Satan will seek to spin every setback, struggle, and sorrow in the direction of unbelief and condemnation. Paul not only describes his struggle as a thorn in the flesh, but also as a messenger of Satan sent to deliver blow after blow to his faith in the Lord and his hope in the gospel. Satan's playbook is predictable and deadly—just lies about God and us. He wants to crowd out the word of God's grace with whispers of doubt and despair. Do these words sound familiar?

- If God is so good, why are you facing this?
- You are a failure!
- You are not good enough.
- No one really loves you.
- Things will never change for the better.
- Jesus is not enough for this.
- This is punishment.

- No one else knows or cares what you are going through.
- God's promises are for everyone but you.

Like a tiny splinter, once embedded and left to do its work, those words will create terrible spiritual infections because what we believe and what we think really does control our world.

Paul and Fiona knew something about that—though they still attended church, it was not the same. The words of the songs and sermons that once delighted them now bounced off without making a dent. Their hunger for spiritual things had given way to a growing spiritual indifference, which only compounded their sense of failure. The Lord seemed to have left them to struggle on their own. Similarly, the words of Satan can quietly sneak in and control our worlds, leaving no room for the Lord to be heard. What satanic voices have you given too much permission to, leaving you feeling like the Lord neither really knows nor cares for you?

The words of self

The average person has more than sixty thousand thoughts per day—an ongoing inner conversation of controlling words that can either reinforce truth or become a distorted voice that unknowingly denies the truth. Paul Tripp puts it vividly when he says, "No one is more influential in your life than you are, because no one talks to you more than you do."[1]

The greatest spiritual battle we face is being fought between our ears. It can get very loud in our heads, so much so that sometimes we wish we could shut it off. The apostle Paul speaks about a particularly difficult time in his ministry when the thoughts of his heart strongly controlled his outlook and emotions: "We were under great pressure, far beyond our ability to endure, so that we despaired of life itself. Indeed, we felt we had received the sentence of death" (2 Corinthians 1:8–9).

As he surveyed his situation and measured it against his own potential, the outlook was bleak. His inner voice, ruminating on the genuine difficulty of what he faced, led to feelings that he was as good as dead. But later he realized that those thoughts and feelings were distorted because they hadn't told him the whole story. He goes on to say that there was more in play than he was thinking about at the time: "But this happened that we might not rely on ourselves but on God, who raises the dead" (2 Corinthians 1:9).

In his struggle he had missed a vital piece—the deeper work of the Lord in his life that was calling him away from self-reliance to faith. The voice of self had influenced him deeply, but had not told him the whole truth.

Paul and Fiona knew something of that—despairing and longing for change, their thoughts were trapped in a cycle of distraction and distortion and pain, preventing them from recognizing the truth they desperately needed to hear. Their understandable craving for relief and release got louder and louder. Each interaction became high jeopardy and made them feel like their very lives were at stake. The voice of Christ seemed almost irrelevant. The words of self were controlling their worlds, leaving no room for the Lord to be heard. What thoughts in yourself have you given too much permission to, leaving you spiraling?

YOU NEED A WORD FROM THE LORD

Recently I watched a clip of a preacher who was addressing a congregation in pain. The preacher said, "I see people with thorns, more than one." But what struck me was what he said next. He could have said many things—perhaps some words of comfort and sympathy. But this is what he said: "We need a word from the Lord."

We need a word from the Lord—whose voice you have heard before when he "called you out of darkness into his wonderful light" (1 Peter 2:9)—and a voice with such authority that you will be sustained through every pain and disappointment. When the Lord declares that "Man shall not live on bread alone, but on every word that comes from the mouth of God" (Matthew 4:4), he really does mean it. His words are literal soul food, without which we spiral into the traps of distorted voices.

And it is a word from the Lord that changed everything for Paul: "But he said to me" (2 Corinthians 12:9).

We are at a strange point in the passage we've been unwrapping because Paul was at the end of himself. He recounts this hugely pivotal spiritual period in his life, and as he looks back and tells the story of the pain that this thorn had brought, Paul shows how sorrow, confusion, disappointment, and an experience of his own weakness had become constant companions. He shows how he has cried out to the Lord, begging him to take it away. He shows how he has poured out his soul to the Lord. We saw something of that in the last chapter, didn't we? He shows how he has cried out for mercy. He shows how he has expressed his sorrow and how he has shouted out, "Lord, do something!" But Paul is the one who has done all the talking. I myself know that tendency to do all the talking before the Lord. Paul had prayed and nothing had changed . . . but it doesn't mean he got nothing. What did he get? He got five words. Did he get what he wanted? What did he get?

"But he said to me . . ."

We can't move on from this. You might ask, "Ste, why are you spending a whole chapter on these five words?" The answer is that this is the whole nine yards of biblical change! This is where hope comes from. The reality that there is One outside of us, who knows us and loves us, who is working out his purposes in Christ to renovate the world, and you, for the glory of Jesus, and who is moving everything in the right direction. What is his means of getting us there? A magic wand?

No. He speaks.

He speaks over nations. He speaks over calamities. He speaks to heavenly authorities. But when he speaks, everything is different—everything.

As we read Paul's words, we get the sense that he is submissively saying, "Hold on; everything stops when the Lord speaks." The Spirit of God called Paul personally and spoke a personal word.

We have those same Spirit-wrought words in the Scriptures that have come to us. Our experiences and life situations might be like Paul's or completely different. But we, too, are called to have the same posture as the apostle—one of listening to the words of him who rules the wind and the sea. We can almost hear Paul saying, "If God is speaking, I want his voice to be the voice I hear the loudest—above all the other voices. I already know what I think, and I already know the limitations of what I can do. But please, O Lord, speak. Your servant listens."

"But he said **to me . . .** " What are the next two words? This is the bit that lights up my heart. I love these next two words: "*to me*"! You really need to get a hold of this because this is at the center of who our living God is. In the Bible we find that God is transcendent, which means he is over all things. He has total authority and is beyond our full comprehension. He is transcendent, but he is immanent. Do you know what "immanent" means? He is close to us. He is powerful and he is personal. He is *over* all things, and he is *involved in* all things. He speaks personally to people.

All of you reading this are the living proof of this, if you know Jesus Christ as your Lord and Savior. There was a day when you were spiritually dark, outside of Christ, listening to the voices of culture, the voice of the enemy, and voices of your own making, but something broke through. What once seemed dull, boring, and insignificant—the voice of the Lord in the Bible—was made alive. The Word of God comes, the Holy Spirit takes a hold of this truth of who he is, and you are shifted, in that moment as you respond in faith, from darkness to light, from death to life, from lostness to eternity—to an inheritance. That's what happens when God's voice breaks in, and that is what goes on happening day after day after day when we know Jesus Christ.

What happens for Paul in this story is no accident. Do you notice the pivotal point for Paul? He has been in anguish, he's had unanswered prayers, he's cried out to the Lord. He is at the end of himself. "I prayed, and nothing changed." I have had countless conversations with people, with circumstances like this in their life, when they've been trying to make sense of things. They feel like it's game, set, and match; there is nothing else. But isn't it strange that—at this point of brokenness, when life has been turned upside down—it's at *this* point that the Lord comes in. "But he said to me . . ."

It is virtually never what people expect they need to hear. Why should we be surprised at that? We should almost be expectant. At that point of pain, moments of revelation are just around the corner. That's what we pray for. This isn't just some sort of mystic moment with a finger pointing out of the sky. No, God speaks to us through ordinary means—his written Word brought to us by the Spirit of the living God.

Do you remember how the Lord Jesus spoke on the night of his betrayal and in the high priestly prayer? He spoke of the Spirit, saying, "But when he, the Spirit of truth, comes, he will guide you into all the truth" (John 16:13). He prayed to the Father, "Sanctify them by the truth; your word is truth" (John 17:17). His prayer reveals *his* expectation. Though it will be Christ who achieves our salvation, it will be through the powerful word of God found in the Bible that we encounter and experience that salvation at work in our lives. That voice of truth about him will set his people apart, sanctify them, and send them out on mission. That's what he is busy doing day after day after day: speaking through his Word to sanctify you by the truth. He knits your circumstances, your moments, and even your points of desperation, sorrow, and confusion together to bring you to a point, in his great wisdom, where his Word will penetrate to a level that's even beyond your expectations. He will make you new.

As we've been seeing through the previous chapters, sorrow and pain have a unique way of revealing our sense of self—all our hopes, our beliefs, and our whole life posture. Guess who owns all of those things? Guess who owns us? He does!

Whose voices have you been listening to? You yourself have had an idea of who you want to be. I might have lots of ideas about what it looks like to be Ste, and some of them, unsurprisingly, are in conflict with the Lord's plan and his good purpose. Who are you going to trust? Whose voice are you going to listen to?

Sometimes, we don't want to lay our hopes down. We think, "This is what I want my life to be about. This is my designer life. This is what I want for the future. Here are some of the things that I have to have. If you haven't given them to me, Lord, or if you've taken some of them away, then I'm going to get really, really angry!" And the Lord comes alongside you, and he says, "Listen, I'll tell you about what true hope is, and it's better than your ideas. I'll speak to you about what you need to put your hope in today."

What about our beliefs? We don't want to lay them down either. I like to think about myself, about God, and about the world on my terms. Have you ever thought about your little construction of what God is like? Your little construction of God, particularly during moments of pain, is strangely similar to whom? You! You want him to be just like you, but like a bigger version of you. You want him to have *your* wisdom. But the Lord says something like, "Actually, I'm a lot better and bigger than that! And perhaps there'll be a moment when you'll be able to receive this. I am going to speak."

"But he said to me . . . " Will that be enough for you? Will that voice be enough? In every encounter with Christ in the Gospels, there is some sort of crisis. He reveals himself to be the King as he speaks a word, and his words reorient everybody around him. Do all people get what they ask for? No. Do all people get better than they ask for? Yes, because they get *him*. He soothes souls, he settles people who are feeling broken, he challenges the stubborn, and he upends and overturns lies and self-sufficiency. He is still doing that very same thing today. His words to his people, to us, are personal and powerful.

OWEN'S STORY—WHAT HAPPENS WHEN GOD SPEAKS

Let me tell you a story about a friend of mine. Owen was in his twenties, tall, athletic, in a high-powered job, and newly married. From the outside, it looked as if he was on top of his world, but the reason we were talking was that his new marriage had crumbled, and his wife had left him. He was overcome with depression and anxiety—so much so that he had taken a leave of absence from work.

His wife had walked out because he wouldn't communicate with her, and she had discovered his long-term love affair with pornography. When I asked him about this, he seemed to see it as just something that he did. I asked him about what his life was like, and about what motivated him, and he said, "Well, I just want to be really good at what I do."

I asked, "So what has gone wrong? Why has she gone?" and he replied, "Because, whenever there is something wrong, I close down, withdraw, and try to escape into a place that just gives me a little bit of comfort." Of course, that place was pornography. He told me that he had prayed, again and again, "Lord, take this struggle away from me." He believed that if that struggle was removed, everything would be OK.

I asked about his identity, saying, "Who are you? Who *are* you?" He described his sporting achievements and his looks; he mentioned his beautiful wife and his excellency in his job. I said, "Well, most of those have been taken away from you. Who are you now?" He answered, "The Bible tells me that I am a child of God." So I asked if that was true for him, and I really appreciated that he was honest enough to say, "I don't really know."

Another thing Owen was good at was knowing the Bible. He really knew a lot about what the Bible has to say about God, about the world, and about himself. He knew plenty of things that were true. But do you know where he kept them? In his head.

I invited him to consider if he was holding certain truths about the Lord (or words the Lord had spoken to him) at a distance. "Could we look in closer? You know that Jesus has forgiven sins and has paid the ultimate price. But do you really know him?"

He said, "I suppose I don't."

I asked again, "You know that Christ has claimed you to himself and has established a righteousness for you; do you *know* him?" He just looked confused, so I challenged him to go to his favorite sections of Scripture, highlight them, and ask what God was saying to him about what God had done for him in Christ and what difference that would make when trying to move forward that week.

The following week, when I next saw him, he looked different! He said he'd found Galatians 2:20, and then he quoted it to me: "I have been crucified with Christ and I no longer live, but Christ lives in me. The life I now live in the body, I live by faith in the Son of God, who loved me and gave himself for me."

There is nothing in this verse about marriage, pornography, or work. What possible good could it do for Owen? But it changed his life. The Lord knows what we need to hear, and usually it's something quite different from what we might have expected—different and better. This word from the Lord for Owen reoriented his whole life. That was the unexpected answer to his prayers.

He told me, "This tells me who I am, and it's not my job, or my looks. It tells me that I'm not the perfect man I'm trying to be. I am so messed up that I need Jesus to come and die and save me and rescue me!"

I asked, "What's happened that made you actually take this in?"

He said, "I started to really listen to God's Word, saying to myself, No, this isn't just some theology I know out there. This is something that God has said to me, and I need to take it in. I kept thinking that in this moment God is speaking to me about himself, inviting me to live out what he has said to me—actually taking it, putting shoes on it, and walking about."

I said, "Tell me about that. How did that impact how you went into work?"

"Well, normally when I go into work, I try and look like I've got it all together, but this week, I confessed to making a mistake!"

I asked, "How did that feel?"

"Terrifying because it felt like I was giving my whole self away—my identity as the one who makes things happen, always trying to control my own life, and being terribly fearful and withdrawing when I don't feel like I measure up."

I said, "Has that battle for identity totally gone?"

"No," he said, "it sounds too easy, but I just let God's truth speak to me, and I prayed as I went toward my supervisor and admitted to a mistake."

I said, "Wow. That's amazing! Tell me about what else it has done."

"Well, I had contact with my estranged wife last week, and rather than just holding her at a distance, I opened up about what I was learning from God's Word. Then I told her something about me and what's really going on inside me. I've never been able to do that before."

"What gave you the safety to do that, then?"

"Well, the Lord has said this to me, and it is reality, and I want to believe him now."

I asked, "What's going to be the next step? You're always trying to look perfect in front of people at work. What's the next step?"

"Well, Jesus Christ came and he secured me in love. Maybe instead of seeing work as a place where I prove my worth and then have the crash when I fail, maybe work is going to be a place where I move out toward loving other people."

I asked about the hospital setting where he worked. "How are you going to do that?"

"Well, I am going to try to talk to other people about how they are doing and actually care."

"Whoa! That's a big change around! Can you tell me next week how that goes?"

He came back to me the following week with two examples. One had gone disastrously, and one had gone beautifully. This guy who was living in a posture of "I know my theology and I keep it out there" was now living what he believed. His collapse and the failure that he had prayed against had been the moment that had turned his life upside down and had revealed to him that he had been living a performance-based life. But that life was crushing him. Without hearing the voice of the Lord, he coped by withdrawing, covering up, and finding comfort in pornography.

"So tell me about the pornography," I requested.

He said, "I haven't been there in the last two weeks."

"Why not? Is it because you knew it was bad?"

"No, I always knew it was bad. It's because I want to hide myself in Jesus Christ, not some images on a screen."

Owen had heard the voice of the Lord. The same voice that calmed the storm at sea, raised the dead to life, and flattened Paul on the road to Damascus—that voice spoke to Owen and worked a deep-down change in him. Instead of listening to all the other voices that were shouting at him, he heard the voice of the Lord.

Do you see the power of God's authoritative and personal Word? We can't live as believers if we don't hear his voice. In the midst of all the competing voices in our heads, in the midst of our disappointments, and in the midst of the bitterness and sadness of a broken world, can we let the Lord have the final word?

WHAT'S GOD'S WORD TO YOU TODAY?

We are simple people, and we can't remember ten things at once. Invariably, if you could remember one vital truth in the moment of trial and then seek your God, you would be different. Bible verses aren't magic, but God's words are revelations *of* God *from* God for our redemption. I love how David Powlison put it:

> What one thing about God in Christ speaks directly into today's trouble? Just as we don't change all at once, so we don't take in all of truth in one massive Bible transfusion.[2]

So stop for a moment and ask Jesus to tell you one thing about God in Christ today in his Word. This is a prayer God will always answer.

If you have been a Christian for any amount of time, then the phrase we have been talking about, "but he said to me," is part of your lived experience, isn't it? Maybe for decades he has upheld you—even if you sometimes wish it were from a more secure position. He will uphold you and keep you through his great and precious promises and the knowledge of him, as the apostle Peter said. In those you have everything you need. Do you really believe that? Believe that his voice is his means of calling and keeping you. In his great and precious promises, and through the knowledge of him, you have everything you need for life and godliness (2 Peter 1:3–4 ESV).

- Except when . . . my prayers aren't answered?
- Except when . . . my most precious relationship gets blown up?
- Except when . . . I lose a loved one?

No. In his great and precious promises, Jesus has given you himself, powerfully and personally. His voice is inviting us into his life, where we are sustained, comforted, and helped—a life where we are hidden in Christ. Ask to hear the voice of Jesus today. He will answer.

A DAILY PRAYER TO HEAR THE VOICE OF JESUS

> Father, thank you that you speak words of life. Forgive me for the ways in which I put off your voice in favor of other ones. In my head, I have run on a track of excuses, rationalization, justifying, and bitterness. I have listened to all the other voices in my life except yours. I have not said, "Down with those voices, and up with yours, Lord." Give me a heart that is eager to have a word from you. Please speak to me what I need to hear even when I am resistant. I want to love your words again. In Jesus's name, Amen.

Chapter 6

HE SUPPLIES

I was heading into a difficult conversation.

Rose had started to live with a non-Christian boyfriend. She was nervous, threatened, and looking for a way out. I talked to her about God's love, kindness, and sufficiency, but she withdrew more and more. I will never forget the look she gave me—resolute and filled with regret. She said, "That's all well and good, Ste, but Jesus can't give me a hug at night."

I'd like to tell you that in that moment I insightfully and gently discerned her heart and unpacked for her the sufficiency of God's grace in a way that was meaningful to her, to her desires for intimacy, connection, and validation, but instead I must be honest and say that in that moment, I found her logic compelling and persuasive.

After all, she had a long time to think about it. It had started months ago with her praying for someone to share her life with. Day by day, she had constructed a mental image of a life that could carry the weight of her soul's deepest longings—something that will get her through. The foundation for that construction was an unstated assumption that the grace of God in Christ was not sufficient for her struggles.

Long before the night we sat down, Rose's faith had been growing—faith not in the sufficiency of God's grace but in her attachment to what she thought would be the only thing that would satisfy her soul. I'd caught wind of it weeks earlier, when she came to church looking withdrawn. I'd asked her what was burdening her, and how I could pray for her, but she responded with cold resignation, "I prayed, but nothing changed." The grace of Jesus Christ that had once lit her up with joy was now feeling dutiful and dull. Where once singing with God's people filled her with hope, she was now distracted by the background hum of emptiness that would linger until she got her Christless version of sufficient grace. Almost imperceptibly, she was turning from the Lord to her new vision. So with a bold move of faith in what she had become convinced would be the only thing that was sufficient, she had taken matters into her own hands.

Has this ever happened to you? It starts with a simple wish, and then before we know it, our imaginings of what could be become the only thing that will be enough for our souls and make us feel whole. So in pastoral conversations, I have taken to asking people my "magic-button question." It is very revealing. It goes something like this: "If right now I could press a 'magic button' that would change one thing for you, what would it be?"

On occasion, it is met with an exasperated sigh and an accompanying facial expression that says, "Haven't you been listening to a word I've said?" But more often than not, my "magic-button question" helps people consider what would be enough to see them through the difficulties of the present moment, especially when people have prayed and nothing has changed. The opportunity to question what we have said would be "enough" or "sufficient for me" is invaluable. It is so easy to look horizontally for a savior. It's so easy to buy into the delusion that sufficiency and "enough" in life can be found outside of the person and work of the Lord Jesus Christ. It is so easy to have as our starting point that God's grace is not sufficient for my struggle. Yet, if we are brave enough to name our "magic button," it opens the door to letting a sufficiency beyond our imagination meet us at our point of need. Rose's "magic button" was, of course, a flesh-and-blood companion who could give her a hug at night.

THE APOSTLE PAUL'S MAGIC BUTTON

Paul too had a magic button that he wished the Lord would press. As he feared his stock would plummet before the eyes of man because of his thorn, his persistent prayers revealed the only thing that he thought would be enough—the removal of his accursed thorn. It's hard to believe that the great apostle would be tempted to believe that the grace he already had in Jesus Christ was not greater than his struggle, yet we must assume this is where his heart was, for what else would explain the Lord's choice of words to him at this turning point? I wonder whether he was initially indignant? I wonder whether, like so many others, this exposing of subtle unbelief led him to feel shame? I wonder whether he just simply struggled to believe?

What was God's personal word for Paul in the midst of trouble? What was the one thing that Paul needed to hear from God? "My grace is sufficient for you" (2 Corinthians 12:9a). Yes, the apostle of grace needed to be challenged by the Lord himself to turn away from any notion that anything other than the sufficiency of God's grace was what his life needed. It's as if the Lord were saying to him, "I have you covered, and more than that, in ways you can barely imagine. You don't need what you think you need. All you need for this moment, and going forward, is the sufficiency of my grace to you."

When the Lord says his grace is sufficient, he does not mean merely adequate or enough but an ongoing supply of "enough-ness" that cannot be exhausted, for the resources of heaven are abundant and inexhaustible. It is not a question of earning this supply, for Christ has done that for us. It is more a question of accessing what is already ours in Christ. We question whether this grace is sufficient for a broken heart, dashed dreams, deep sorrow, and spiraling disappointment—when our very identity is under assault, and we are emotionally spent. This is where Paul was. Yet the end of the story for Paul was not "God's grace is less than my struggles," for why else would he tell this story? And though he is in a low place, the glorious end to his battle with unanswered prayer is a resounding "God's grace IS greater than my struggles!" His grace truly is enough for every moment.

Jesus invites you to go on this journey too. He supplies you with grace enough for the life he has called you to. Can you identify where on this journey you are right now?

Perhaps you are only just now realizing that you have a "magic button." You are desperate and pleading that God would provide you with your version of enough-ness because the grace of Jesus doesn't feel like enough right now. You feel weak and cannot see any good coming out of it. From your vantage point, it feels like a disaster, but from the vantage point of heaven, everything is going according to plan. The unwanted weakness you feel is positioning you to receive more than you had hoped for. God has to expose the objects of our faith that have taken his place. This is what author Paul Tripp calls "uncomfortable grace."

> I think there are many times when we are going through those kinds of things and we cry out, "Where is the grace of God?" All the time, however, we are, in fact, receiving the grace of God. But it's not the grace of relief, nor is it the grace of release. Relief will come some day—release will come some day—but what you actually need now is the grace of refinement. We must, in light of eternity, begin to teach and comfort and encourage one another with the "theology of uncomfortable grace." Very often, this side of eternity, God's grace comes to you in uncomfortable forms—because that's exactly what you need.[1]

The discomfort comes in questioning, and then ultimately letting go of, our magic buttons. Is it reasonable to expect the Lord to bring the sufficiency of his grace into a life that has its faith elsewhere? This is uncomfortable because it is a battle for what rules your heart. Like Rose, you have become very attached to your version of "enough-ness," and perhaps, like Paul, you are still clinging to the hope that the Lord will simply capitulate and give you your version of grace. Yet he loves you too much to give you anything less than "my grace."

Perhaps you are further on in this journey and are open to hearing the Lord say to you, "My grace is sufficient for you." You are wondering how this claim connects to your life and struggle right now. You are willing to consider surrendering your magic button, but it's hard to give it up when that button feels so tangible, while on the other hand, his grace feels so ethereal and remote. Be encouraged that this is the only place anyone has ever found grace. It is when the Lord meets us in the low place that things start to turn around, and that is by design.

Wherever you are, the medicine is going to be the same—to look again, much like Paul was forced to, at the sufficiency of God's grace. What does God's grace bring to us? When the Lord says "my grace," there are at least three vital components he is referring to—his pursuit, his provision, and his power.

THE PURSUIT OF GRACE

When we pursue our magic buttons, we can become blind to how the Lord is pursuing us. I don't think many believers set out to be apathetic about the grace of God toward them. Apathy just quietly slides in, like a silent, deadly virus that incubates in our hearts. Before we realize it, the life-giving hope of God's grace-filled pursuit of us has been eclipsed and belittled by the pains and demands of the moment. Our pursuit of relief redefines in our minds what it means for God to be gracious, and then getting answers to the pleadings of our hearts becomes our central aim.

When Paul starts his letter to the Corinthians with the greeting of "Grace and peace to you from God our Father and the Lord Jesus Christ," he is not uttering an empty platitude, but summarizing the entirety of the Bible about the heart of God toward sinners and sufferers. The grace of God is how he pursues the needy and undeserving, pursuing them for their good. Or, as pastor David Mathis points out,

> The grace of God is on the loose. . . . the grace of God is turning the world upside down. God is shamelessly pouring out his lavish favor on undeserving sinners of all stripes and thoroughly stripping away our self-sufficiency.[2]

This is "grace to you," and if you are a believer today, your story, up to this point, is living proof of that reality, for his grace found you when you were not looking for him. As Dane Ortlund points out,

> We lose sight not just of him, but the sense of what lengths he went to save us. When we were running full speed in the opposite direction, he chased us down, subdued our rebellion, and opened our eyes to see our need of him and all his sufficiency to meet our need. We were not drowning in need of a life preserver, but stone-dead at the bottom of the ocean. He pulled us up and breathed new life into us, and sets us on our feet.[3]

Do you need new life breathed into you? He has done it before and can do it again. Do you need setting on your feet? Then you are perfectly positioned, for his grace is attracted to weakness and moves in the direction of those in need. He didn't save you to leave you to your own devices. He is pursuing you right now. This is the "grace to you" that Paul wants the Corinthians to say is more than enough for their struggle, just as it turned out to be for him: "Though I was distracted by the thorn, pursuing my version of enough-ness, this grace was pursuing after me." Could that be enough for you too?

I will never forget the look of renewed hope on the face of a recovering addict from our church as we discussed this grace. She had experienced some very dark moments of failure and felt totally stuck. I asked her what changed. "I started to believe that God's grace was bigger than my struggle," she replied. Knowing the painful details of her story, I wanted to hear what that meant for her. What she said is etched in my memory. Her reply was glorious in its vivid simplicity: "No matter how big a pit I dig myself into, I know that he has got a bigger shovel."

It might be hard for you right now if you, like my friend, are in a pit that you can see no way out of. You have determined what you need from God, and can't understand why you have prayed but nothing has changed. But what if he has a bigger shovel? What if he *is* the bigger shovel, and he is coming for you? He did it before when you were lost in your sin and has no intention of forgetting about you now. He can't because he is "the God of all grace" (1 Peter 5:10), but that will only light you up if you know you need that more than anything else.

Paul thought he couldn't live with his thorn in the flesh. He thought that he couldn't live without the relief from pain that was his magic button. Instead, he discovered that the only thing he could not live without was the gracious pursuit of the living God. Put simply, independent of Paul's senses and feelings in the moment, God's grace kept showing up for him.

I wish there was an easier way, but there isn't—you can only discover the infinite value of this grace when you have nothing left. When you can't find him, or when you can't hold on to him, that is exactly when the pursuing grace of God becomes the most valuable. It is his pursuit of me that is sufficient when I have nothing but a broken heart and a confused mind.

Consider this: perhaps your painful experiences with seemingly unanswered prayer are clearing the way for a fresh revelation of Jesus's sufficient supply of grace. He isn't asking you to be well put together, to have all the right answers, or to be deserving—that's the point: you're not and you can't be. The wonder of this pursuing grace of God is that he meets you right where you are right now. Perhaps you have been forced to see yourself as much more needy and hopeless than you ever dared consider before. This is God's grace to you. Though your need might have surprised you, it has not surprised him, and his response is to pursue you again, pursuing with more "grace to you."

Imagine if Rose would reopen her heart to this supply. I don't doubt a hug at night is meaningful, comforting, and affirming. But in comparison with the security, the potential, and the vitality of Jesus coming for you again and again, it is woefully insufficient. Her "enough" is exposed as actually very little. Could she dare to see the Lord's gracious pursuit of her as more operative in her life than any current difficulty, loss, or disappointment? That is the supply of "my grace."

Is this a door you can walk through? Can you, right now, lay aside your magic button, your plans, and your future hopes and say to Jesus, "I trust you to pursue me in just the right way. Make that enough for me. Only you can do this"?

This is a prayer that Jesus will always answer with a yes.

HIS PROVISION—"IS SUFFICIENT FOR YOU"

The amazing thing about grace is that even though God owes us nothing, he delights to give us everything. Yet we rarely sense or see it because we are looking for the wrong indicators of it in the wrong places. Perhaps, looking at the evidence of your life right now, you would be tempted to believe that the grace of God does not provide much of value, and that he has passed you by. Paul could have concluded that, if the answer to his pleadings were the sole measure of the provision of God's grace. But that is to look in the wrong place. We have to fix our eyes elsewhere: "So we fix our eyes not on what is seen, but on what is unseen, since what is seen is temporary, but what is unseen is eternal" (2 Corinthians 4:18).

Maybe you have cried out in desperation to God, "Why haven't you provided for my life?" And though we don't expect an answer, when we really look at the life and death of the Lord Jesus Christ, we find he is quietly speaking back to us: "I did provide, I am providing, and I always will provide for you more than you can imagine." This unseen, sufficient grace is nothing short of the totality of redemption and new life won for you by Christ. It is the grace of God authoring an intervention that transforms your life through the gospel of his Son. You are rich beyond measure because of this gracious provision.

Paul explains it like this: "For you know the grace of our Lord Jesus Christ, that though he was rich, yet for your sake he became poor, so that you through his poverty might become rich" (2 Corinthians 8:9). This is what grace objectively gives you, at no cost to you, but immeasurable cost to Christ. The superior one is granting to us, the inferior ones, what we cannot earn and would never be able to repay. As a Christian, you are "in Christ," and it is of such worth to be found in him that this grace alone is enough for any moment of life, no matter how difficult. In fact, the more difficult the moment, the more precious the grace will become to us because it is eternal and enduring.

Living out of God's unseen provision

Magic-button moments present opportunities for us to ask questions about who we imagine ourselves to be and what we believe our lives should contain. But so often we discover that those imaginings are strangely devoid of new life in Christ. This may surprise us, but it doesn't surprise the Lord. He knows that we all have a drift toward the seen over the unseen. He knows where we try to find life and identity, what we wish we had or could be, and how much those things are a cheap counterfeit of what we already have through the grace of Christ. He sees how our strivings to have these things are exhausting us and robbing him of the glory that is rightly due to him. He knows that his provision is more substantial and enduring than any other comfort, sense of self, or life that we could look to.

And here we come to the crux of the matter—why we need a grace that is sufficient. I begin to realize that I need grace not only to get me through this thorny period but also because of what the thorn reveals in me. I feel deeply the ways that I am trying to live based on things that are seen, instead of the unseen provisions and riches of the gospel. And I'm in a fight. I learn about the many ways I am resistant to living purely by grace.

I appreciated the honesty of a dear friend when he admitted as much. He was not someone who struggled to name his magic buttons, and he was deeply dismayed when the Lord did not give him what he had hoped to find security in.

He confessed, "I'm living through targeted strikes at what is holding me back from living purely out of his grace. I know I shouldn't want them, but there are things I just want more than the grace of God." I invited him to consider what the end of the story would be. "I suppose if he really loves me, he won't let up until I stop fighting back against his provision of grace," he replied. And without realizing it, he had so casually stated what is so amazing about grace. While the tendency of the human heart is to fix our eyes on and fight for seen things like our magic buttons, the Lord is fighting for us to fix our eyes on and fight to live based on the glorious unseen realities of Christ's victories. All seen things are temporary and will fail us eventually, but our new life in Christ is eternal and unshakable.

This means that contrary to your initial assumptions, this thorny period is not the Lord withholding grace from you but holding his provision of grace out to you with fresh vigor. He wants you to be so fixed on what is unseen that you are forever changed.

Is this a door that you can walk through right now? Are you willing to swap your confidence in your hoped-for magic button for what Jesus has already provided—himself? Can you say to Jesus, "Help me see you. Help me to see what's more real than all that I wish this life could bring me. Forgive me for looking for life apart from your grace."

This is a prayer that Jesus will always answer with yes.

HIS POWER—"IS MADE PERFECT IN WEAKNESS"

Can you see that all of what we have talked about here is how God's power is made perfect in weakness? Turning away from your magic buttons will make you feel weak. That thing you don't believe you can live without is what you are hoping will make you feel strong and complete. But it is not as strong as the grace of God. When we are stripped of our magic buttons, when we are feeling weak and worn, when we turn to the Lord—that's when his power is made perfect.

This is the Lord's declaration of intent for your life. He wants to write power into your life—not your power but his power. The word that Paul uses for "power" is the root word for *dynamite*. God's power is like dynamite, but even stronger. It's so powerful that it will loosen your hold on all that keeps us from him.

The power God gives is for his good purposes in our life, not to fulfill our plans and life goals. It's power to live for him in every moment. It's not a grace to be who I want to be, to have life according to my preferences, or to pursue my vision for personal happiness. It's a powerful grace at work, so that I can be who God has called me to be in Christ for his glory and my ultimate good. This is what his powerful grace is working to do. Despite my hesitancy, and even despite my reluctance, his grace will be sufficient to make me complete and completely new. And the only way you experience that is by coming to the end of yourself. That's the weakness part.

But the dynamite part is that there will be supernatural things that happen when God gives us his strength to walk in faith in the midst of struggle. God doesn't just tell us to do something—he gives us power to do it. Paul, based on long experience with his weakness and God's power, says, "God is able to make all grace abound to you" (2 Corinthians 9:8 ESV). Jesus is able and willing to effect a change within your very heart that transforms your capacity to endure, be gracious, serve, and obey.

To have "all grace abound to you" is to have the work of Jesus personally applied to the unfolding story of your life in the midst of difficult moments, unwanted situations, and unmet desires. Once broken, we become whole again; once selfish and insecure, we become self-giving and stable. His grace is sufficient to reclaim you for his very own, rewiring your heart so that it becomes a heart like his.

Time and again, mirroring the testimony of Paul about the sufficiency of God's grace, believers have found that their biggest breakthroughs with the Lord have come when their own weakness was most apparent.

But what does it actually look like to enter in, to lean in to God's abounding, dynamite grace? It starts by looking out for a different kind of power at work in your life than what your magic button offers you. Consider what happened to my friend Bill as he headed into a lengthy prison sentence. He was terrified of the potential physical threats from angry, out-of-control inmates. Having never been in a fight, he simply didn't want to get beaten up. Desperate to keep his head down, he realized that despite being vigilant and careful with what he said, he was very much at the mercy of the other prisoners' moods and cruelty. Daily he would pray for safety, wanting the power of God's providence to deliver him from what his own weakness could not prevent. He was genuinely, and understandably, afraid.

Partway through his sentence I received a call from him: "Ste, it finally happened yesterday. I've been in my first fight." Both fearing for his physical well-being and concerned that he might feel bitter toward the Lord for not using his power to protect him from this, I asked him how he was doing. His reply was surprisingly upbeat: "Two guys jumped me, and I didn't do a very good job of defending myself. I'm sore and stiff, but strangely encouraged."

This made little sense to me, so I asked him to explain. He told me, "I've been praying for two things while being inside: first, God's power for protection, and second, to be more dependent on his grace to make me new. It was only through what happened yesterday that I realized I can't have the second while I'm clinging to the first. I don't want to get beaten up again, but I can see more clearly now that I am in God's hands, and he has given me a heart to pray for those who attacked me."

His words allowed me to see something the world rarely does—where real power lies. Was it in the hands of the ones who threw the punches, or the one who threw up the prayers for them? Who looked strong and secure, and who was actually strong and secure? Grace was abounding to Bill in ways that he had not been looking for, but, in hindsight, God's grace was unmistakable. My friend would not have been able to experience this had he not been confronted with his weakness.

The promise of God's power is not a promise that he will sprinkle fairy dust on every difficult moment or simply cause them to disappear. But in the midst of every difficulty, he will be working within you to bring about a new you in the image of Jesus. This is the power of grace. By its sufficiency you will stand during struggle, fight off sin, love your neighbor, pray for enemies, and rejoice through trials. Your magic button can't do that, but grace can. Just ask Bill.

This is the enough-ness of his supply of grace.

DAILY PRAYER FOR HIS SUPPLY OF GRACE

> Thank you, Lord, that your grace is greater than my struggles. Forgive me for the ways I look to other things to give me what only new life in Christ can. Without your gracious pursuit, I would be lost. Give me eyes fixed on your unseen riches, and let your grace abound to me in my weakness.

Chapter 7

HE ABIDES

Ricky felt anything but powerful. Battling with loneliness and regret after a painful relationship breakup, he longed to move past it and live with a sense of the nearness of Christ, as he had done when he first came to faith in Jesus. But that was a distant memory. In its place, fear and condemnation were living rent-free in his head from the moment that he woke up to past the point of closing his eyes as he tried and failed to fall asleep. He did not want to be like this—he was angry at himself that he could not push past it and felt ashamed that he was not a better Christian.

"I used to not be like this, but after the breakup I just went downhill." As I spoke with Ricky, I tried to see past his look of misery and imagine what he was like before. With the somber look of someone who felt lost in the dark, he spoke about the lingering, but distant, memories of walking closely with Christ through both joys and trials. His days were marked by a conscious awareness of abiding with God though Christ, but now that felt out of reach. He was even beginning to doubt that they had ever been real at all.

Perhaps you have found yourself in a place like this. You don't want to be here, but hard circumstances and the pursuit of your passions have led you to a barren place spiritually. You say, with Ricky, "I can't believe that the God of all grace would want me to live like this." Do not give way to despair, but be encouraged because you are right.

The wonder of the gospel that Paul has been unpacking to the Corinthian church carries God's power with it for us. "But we have this treasure in jars of clay to show that this all-surpassing power is from God and not from us" (2 Corinthians 4:7). When Paul says "all-surpassing power," he is not talking about the kind of power that gives you superhuman strength for a short period and then fades, but the ongoing renewal and empowering that comes from being in conscious fellowship with God. This fellowship is possible because "God is faithful, who has called you into fellowship with his Son, Jesus Christ our Lord" (1 Corinthians 1:9).

If you are in Christ, he has come into your life, and his Spirit lives in you. He is presently abiding with you and in you. The Christian life does not reach its high point in knowing stuff about God; rather, the true goal is to know and abide with God. Jesus wants to meet you where you are to bring you into his grace, love, and fellowship.

Yet, for us (just like with Ricky), when hard situations have pierced us like a thorn, the conscious awareness of Christ being present and abiding with us is crowded out by distracting thoughts and emotions. The hard situations that are the occasion for seemingly unanswered prayer take over our lives like unwanted squatters. Taking up residence in our thoughts and emotions, they begin a remodeling process that we don't want, often leaving our lives unrecognizable and barely tolerable. Ricky had tried to tell them to go away, but the more he put up a fight, the more they seemed to remain, abide, and rest upon him. Abiding in Christ was a thing of the past.

It's not like he hadn't prayed, but when he prayed, he was simply wanting to feel better: "I know that he promises me that his grace is sufficient, but I just can't push through to it. All I can see is what I have lost, and my life is unbearable. I have prayed, but nothing has changed."

How about you? Do you, like Ricky, know in your head that God's grace is sufficient, but you can't experience it or feel it?

He described to me his daily experience of trying to turn toward Christ: "I open my Bible to read God's Word, but this thorn is there, lingering. I try to close my eyes to turn my heart toward Jesus, but within seconds, I'm distracted back to the thorn in my thoughts. My fears camp out there, and I can't escape their presence. I sort of know that Christ is greater than my problems, but I can't see past my problems to God being with me."

As I listened, it was not hard to relate to his sadness because I have been there many times myself. I did not want to be there, but I simply did not know how to get past the unwanted situation that had exposed my weakness and inadequacy. I would pray, "Help me to know that you are more present and more gracious than this thing that I can't see past." But too often it felt like my attention would quickly drift back to sorrow, or worry, or anger, or despair. I was living with those feelings and the scaffold of distorted thoughts they were built upon, and it felt like the power of Christ had moved away. I suspect that you know something of that struggle too. Is there a way through?

SEE THROUGH, NOT PAST

I was a teenager when a 3D engineer designed what we now call *magic eye pictures*. For a while they became all the rage, since people would compete to find the best one to confound the most people. They work by manipulating a repeating pattern to control the perceived depth and hide a three-dimensional image in a two-dimensional pattern. Behind the pattern lay beautiful vistas—of constellations, marine vessels, or even farmyard scenes—anything that would pop off the page in glorious 3D.

But I couldn't see those images. I would take a look, find that all I could see was the confusing 2D image, and wonder what all the fuss was about. For a while I actually suspected it was a massive hoax and my friends were simply part of a media conspiracy to make me feel useless and look like an idiot. Try as I might, I could not get through what was right in front of me. For what seemed like hours I would gaze, glare, or grimace at the patterns, determined to find what was behind them. Much to the amusement of my friends, I remained defeated, unable to see past the pattern.

That was the case until a rather geeky boy sidled up to me in one first-period math lesson and changed my perspective. "You're doing it wrong. You're trying to see past it. You need to see through it." Now, that made no sense to me, but I was intrigued. So I asked him to explain. "Stop hating the pattern. You have to be aware of the pattern, seeing through it to what is behind it. The pattern helps you see what is through it." To this day, I can't tell you what clicked, but as I squinted once again at the pattern, still aware that it was there but seeing through it, a tiny image began to come into focus. It was only small at first, drifting in and out of perception. But slowly, a 3D world of a beautiful sunrise over a mountain village came into view. Moments earlier, I had been abiding in a world of an unwanted 2D pattern; the next moment, I was aware of a glorious world that had been closer than I realized. As unwanted as the pattern was, I had to look through it to abide in a better reality.

I wonder if you can see where I am going with this. Paul has heard the Lord speak tenderly and determinedly of a present grace through which he will not just endure but experience more than enough sufficiency for any moment. In short, Christ is with him in power. But that gracious word needs to be responded to. We find that he has arrived at a fork-in-the-road moment, marked by a huge decision point. Which way will he go? The outward situation remains unchanged, and he is staring at a life pattern where all he can see are his weakness and unanswered prayer. The situation that he faced was like the dots and squiggles of the 2D pattern that I could not see past—a pattern that stole his joy and cast doubt on the present care and power of Christ. He was living in that pattern—at the whim of voices of doubt, resentment, and fear telling him he was out of options, and there was nowhere else to go and nothing else to see. If Ricky could rewrite Paul's words to the Corinthians, it might have sounded like this: "Disregarding God's promise of grace, I will grumble all the more resentfully about my losses, leaving me to abide with my miserable, impotent self." Have you ever been stuck like that? You will find that the way out is by going through.

For Paul went through to find that his Lord was indeed present in power. Paul's journey with unanswered prayer would not be the breaking of him, but the making of him. Though the satanic intention was to leave Paul abiding in a miserably debilitating 2D pattern of frustration and self-pity, Paul was convinced that these very struggles are the way through to a deeper experience of abiding in Christ. Here was where he took his stand of faith, not trying to move past his struggle but move through his struggle to a deeper abiding in Christ: "Therefore I will boast all the more gladly about my weaknesses, so that Christ's power may rest on me" (2 Corinthians 12:9b).

WE ABIDE AS WE BELIEVE THROUGH WEAKNESS AND STRUGGLE

When coming to new life in Christ for the first time, we must believe that Jesus is bigger than our need. The occasion for that for every new believer is a powerful awareness of our insufficiency. Ricky detailed for me what brought him to Christ in the first place. He grew up in a home that was strict and impersonal. Struggles were never spoken of openly, and failure was met with more emotional distance. Painfully aware that he did not measure up, Ricky longed to be accepted and secure, but, fearing that same kind of failure would occur spiritually, he initially turned down many warm offers to look at Christ.

When one of Ricky's friends became a Christian, he began to hope that Jesus could also be for him. But at the same time, he was realizing that his problems were bigger than he had thought. As he began to understand the person of Christ through his Word, Ricky was struck by an awareness of his powerlessness to provide an answer to his sin, a realization of the emptiness of a life built on the kingdom of self, and a terrible sense that he was missing out on the life he was made for with God. He now felt his weakness even more acutely through a growing awareness of his insufficiency before God.

It would have been easy to stay there, on that side of the 2D impenetrable pattern, enduring the misery that it brought. But instead it became the occasion for a glorious discovery. As Ricky pushed through his fears and inadequacies, the world where Jesus Christ is present and reigning over all that Ricky had no answer for slowly came into increasing clarity.

The word that Paul uses, which is translated "rest on me" or "abide with me," is related to the verb used to describe the shekinah glory of God dwelling in the Most Holy Place of the tabernacle. There the fullness of God's grace, goodness, and power was present visibly with his people. Paul is pointing out that Christ is always present with his people, but, although this point is always true, our awareness and experience of that presence is uniquely available to us when we are positioned to reach out for it. Paul's struggles were the occasion for him to become aware of the immensity of who had personally made himself available to him. As Ricky would find out, his own struggles would also become the occasion for him to experience the presence of Christ in a deeper way.

JESUS IN THE STORM

This was not something new that Paul discovered. This is how God has always abided with his people. His strength is for weak people who know they are weak. Remember the famous story of Jesus calming the storm? The disciples were all too aware of the potential of the storm to ruin them. Jesus, it seemed, was uncaring—sleeping while they were terrified (Mark 4:35–41). As with so many of the hardships and difficulties we face, the storm exposed their powerlessness as it claimed their full attention and consumed their emotions. They abided in a meltdown while remaining oblivious to who abided with them in the boat. The storm did more than expose their powerlessness; it exposed their lack of belief in Christ's power with them.

We know how the story ends. The disciples discover that the only thing more frightening than traveling in a small boat in a monstrous storm is traveling in a small boat in a monstrous storm next to someone who has the authority and power to flatten that thunderstorm with the words, "Peace, be still." But they never would have had a *personal* experience with his present power if they had not had to go through this storm. He dragged them through so they would draw near. Having been forced to reckon with Jesus *through* this stormy experience, they are left staggered: "Who is this? Even the winds and the waves obey him!" (Mark 4:41).

This is not an offer for just a few believers; this is the work of the One who is presently abiding with each of his children. Even when we are stuck—caught up with our stormy thoughts and emotions—he is working to drag us through to enjoy more of who he really is. As we push through the 2D world where we abide, we are ushered into a 3D world where Christ reigns. He wants us to abide there with him.

No wonder, then, that the apostle Paul declares, "I will boast all the more gladly about my weaknesses so that the power of Christ might rest on me." His experience with unanswered prayer has been the occasion to abide more with Christ. He dared to believe, to reach out again with renewed hope, to push through the 2D picture into the 3D world where Jesus's present power becomes experience. Would Ricky do the same? How about you? Can you ask Jesus for renewed faith so that you can trust that this terrible thorny season has uniquely positioned you to experience Christ's presence?

ABIDING THROUGH DESIRING CHRIST

Staring down his battle with the thorn, Paul had no choice but to reevaluate what he wanted most in life. On what would or should he bet his life and worth? Our most desperate prayers reveal those things. And gradually we find a shift away from what we are asking to whom we are asking. We are forced to decide what we want most: what we are asking for or the One we are asking it of. That process was the end point of the story for Paul. He had to decide every day whether "Christ's power resting on me" was just one among many desires or his chief desire.

Would Ricky go on the same journey to make the Lord his chief desire? The 2D pattern of his regret, relational wreckage, and future implications of those issues had become all-consuming. His desire for his lost relationship to be restored had come to rule over his heart. Would he allow me to question what he longed for most?

The desires that rule in our heart can feel overpowering and undeniable, yet the gentle call of Jesus is stronger. He is calling to us in the questioning that comes up in our struggles and thorny experiences. The promise of Christ's power residing with us is breathtaking in its intimacy and scope. He is saying, in effect, "I want to go with you, go to work with you, go into times of solitude with you, go through painful moments with you—I will never leave you." The One who stilled the storm is with us. But our experience of his presence will be affected by whether Jesus is what we want or desire above other things.

The Lord gives us some helpful instruction in the prophecies he gave to Jeremiah. Although this is initially directed to the exiled people of Israel, it applies to us as well. The Lord says, "You will seek me and find me when you seek me with all your heart" (Jeremiah 29:13). Making abiding with Jesus our chief desire is not possible when we are not seeking him wholeheartedly, when we are clinging to the desire to abide with other things, and when we won't loosen our grip on those longings. If we wish to experience him abiding with us by his grace, then we can, but it will only happen as we give him his rightful place. Do you want to abide with him?

How did this work for Ricky? He wanted Jesus, but he was afraid that Christ would not be enough. What he was looking at was a stacked-up set of questions about his present life—his fears for the future, his shame over past failures, his confusion about his worth, and his desire for a relationship that would carry him into his old age. What was he without that? All these things filled his mind's eye; he was stuck abiding there.

ABIDING ONE DAY AT A TIME

Ricky and I spent a lot of time talking about what it would look like to abide in Christ one day at a time. Rather than staring at his circumstances each day while regretting the past and fearing the future, he learned to look to Christ for daily help in his time of need. Instead of trying to figure out how to get through his whole life, and being overwhelmed by the complexity of what he feared might be ahead of him, he asked Jesus for help with each day's troubles—one day at a time.

We talked about the Israelites in the desert and the manna principle that the Lord taught them. Bread rained from heaven every day, but they could only gather enough manna for each day. They tried to gather more, but it just turned moldy and disgusting (Exodus 16). They were just like Ricky, who also wanted tomorrow's supply today. In many ways Ricky's prayer for deliverance was asking God to give him tomorrow's bread today. But that wouldn't be true faith, would it? Putting all your faith in Christ requires a daily dependence on his grace, abiding afresh every day in dependence upon him. Jesus called himself the Bread of Life. He wants us to know that he is enough for today, but he also won't give you tomorrow's supply today.

I dared Ricky to believe that the bread of abiding with Jesus was going to be enough for him—one day at a time. He looked unsure, but when I met with him a week later, he was like a new guy. He said to me, "I have had to look through my circumstance to see Jesus each day." He found himself to be more optimistic, more comforted, and even more self-giving in social situations. He had even asked a Christian friend to pray for him—something he had never done before. He said, "Wanting to meet with Jesus every day has transformed every day. My problems are the same, but I am different."

As he told me this, I was reminded of that mysterious confession of the apostle Paul:

> We are hard pressed on every side, but not crushed; perplexed, but not in despair; persecuted, but not abandoned; struck down, but not destroyed. . . . Therefore we do not lose heart. Though outwardly we are wasting away, yet inwardly we are being renewed day by day. (2 Corinthians 4:8–9, 16)

Situations pressed in on Paul, but they forced him to dwell with Christ until he could confess that however the pressure is pushing in, that pressure will not crush him to destruction, for Christ will never let that happen. Paul takes each seemingly defeating moment as an opportunity to taste afresh the present power of Jesus. He sees through the thorny weakness to all that is sufficient in the grace of Christ. That is what happens when you desire to abide in Christ through your suffering with seemingly unanswered prayer, facing one new day at a time, depending on Jesus to be with you and supply what you need for the demands of that day.

Ricky, by faith, was learning to abide in Christ one day at a time. He was even excited about it. He took a step of faith and turned to Jesus each day for the bread he needed to sustain him—God's sustaining grace. And he found that Jesus was waiting for him. Jesus was with him. And that didn't change his circumstances, but it changed everything about how Ricky lived in those circumstances.

LEARNING TO BOAST IN WEAKNESS

Boasting was an important part of ancient warfare. Imagine the scene as terrified soldiers, wishing desperately that they did not have to face the ordeal that was coming upon them, stepped up to form battle lines. But then the king would lift his voice in a great boast: "We have the greatest army; we are the strongest; we have got what it takes; we can do it." The boast was to get them ready to charge—a taunt of strength and confidence for those who feared they were done for.

Here Paul turns the idea of boasting on its head. His experience with the thorn—of praying and nothing changing—has given him a new boast. His battle has been against needing to be strong in the eyes of the world. So he taunts supposed worldly strength: "Yes, I am weak. Yes, I have been exposed as not having strength. I haven't got what it takes. I can't do it or get through it . . . but the worst you can do will just cast me more into the abiding love of Jesus."

This is a huge turnaround. He has gone from pleading for the relief and removal of the afflicting thorn to gladly boasting in what the thorn has exposed. Despair has been transfigured into delight. The thorn is real, present, and sharp, but it is no longer laying claim to being the controlling influence in his life. He still does not like it, but he is not scared of it like he used to be. It has led him to abide with Jesus more. He boasts in the weakness,

"I am free to live with the reality that I am not enough because Christ's power rests upon me. I'm living based on that now."

When I saw Ricky next, he had learned to boast. He reported how he had unexpectedly caught sight of his former flame across a crowded room. In an instant, all the emotions of the breakup flooded him. Insecurities, failures, and a piercing despair whirled through his mind. Feeling alone and vulnerable, he started rushing toward the door, but, stopping short, he remembered his Bible reading from earlier that day, Psalm 63:8: "My soul clings to you; your right hand upholds me."

"What am I doing?" he asked himself. "Christ is present, and he will powerfully uphold me; do I believe that or not?" He taunted his own insecurities: "I didn't want this to happen, but now that it has, it has given me the chance to lean into the comfort of knowing I am not alone. Jesus is present with me and upholding me to act in faith and love."

And, much to his surprise, he started moving in the direction of the person who had torn his heart to shreds. This is the power of Christ abiding with us as we push through the thorn to see what he wants us to base our lives on.

Where on earth does the glory of God dwell in power? It is in people that are needy and at their end—people that have given up on believing that they can be the hero of their story or that their dreams of a designer life will deliver. So God's glory abides—his power to strengthen sits over, rests upon, and meets with people in the lowly place of acknowledged weakness and need. To get there, like Paul, we have to stare through the disappointments, dead dreams, and aching hearts—through the breaking of our wills and our pursuit of vain glories—at the person of Christ waiting to meet with us in power. Dimly at first, as we see the hazy contours of his sufficient grace, but with deepening clarity, comfort, and satisfaction, he comes into view. And our hearts are bolstered, comforted, and strengthened even as we boast in the weaknesses that have forced us in his direction. If it has not already, this will be your direction of travel, for Jesus is intent on abiding with you.

How are you doing at staring through your weakness to find a strength in Christ? I warn you: you will not feel strong; rather, it will be terribly unsettling, and for much of the time, you will be striving to wriggle free of your weakness. Whether it is emotional, relational, physical, or anything else, no one likes to walk with a limp. But if we stare through the complicated pattern of sorrow—facing our inabilities, feeling inadequate, and feeling incompetent for the demands of the moment—we will find the precious mercy and the faithfulness of God in Christ. This won't be merely theoretical, but personal and experiential, for Christ came not merely to help us learn about his strength, but to reveal his strength in our weakness. He meets people like me and people like you.

Joni Eareckson Tada has to face, and then stare through, that weakness every day, following her diving accident as a teenager that left her a quadriplegic. She says about her fifty years of paralysis,

> I have learned that the weaker we are, the more we need to lean on God; and the more we lean on God, the stronger we discover him to be. It never

> would have happened had God not given me the bruising of the blessing of that wheelchair.[1]

I'm sure that the apostle Paul would hear of her struggle and her strength and say, "That's what I'm talking about." That's what it means to boast all the more gladly of your weakness so that the power of Christ might abide with us.

This is the way that your thorn is not only robbed of its power but also becomes the confusing puzzle through which wonderful things come into view. Here is the answer to the question, "How can I be OK when I'm not OK?" We are ultimately OK in any situation that positions us to abide more deeply with Jesus. His mercies are new every morning. There is bread from heaven available and waiting every new day so that each day we can get up and do it again.

A PRAYER FOR ABIDING WITH JESUS

> Thank you, Lord, that you are abiding closer to me than I realize right now. Forgive me that my mind and emotions so often want to be stuck abiding on my pains and disappointment. Help me to push through the storm to find you. Help me to want you above all else. Do such a work in me that I taunt my difficulties and disappointments, for they have been the occasion to abide more closely with my Savior. You are all the daily bread I need.

Chapter 8

I PRAYED AND EVERYTHING CHANGED

I'll never forget when a lady dashed up to speak to me at church after we had celebrated the baptism of a number of new believers. Before going into the baptism pool they had each read out a carefully thought-through testimony of how the Lord, through sometimes deeply painful experiences, had upended their lives and self-sufficiency, and then, in equally unexpected ways, had brought them to delight in his salvation. They each spoke of personal experiences of the grace of Jesus meeting them, forgiving them, and holding them. It seemed that despite the painful path they had walked, for them, the destination had been more than worth it, and they were overflowing with praise.

They were not accomplished speakers, but there was a remarkable power in their ordinary personal testimonies of Jesus's grace in their lives. In all their testimonies, their weakness contrasted with the strength they spoke about finding in Christ. He was being made manifest in their new life with him.

The lady in question, deeply moved by what she had seen and heard, was trying to understand what had brought them to this point and how she might get there herself. "When will I know I am ready to be baptized?" she asked. I could have simply replied, "Repent and be baptized. . . in the name of Jesus Christ" (Acts 2:38), but wanting to answer in keeping with what she had seen, I found myself saying, "When you have a testimony that surprises you and moves you to praise—of Jesus unmaking and remaking you so you begin to echo his life pattern." After all, that is what to expect on a journey with Jesus. A nervous look broke over her face as the ultimate reality of the Christian life started to dawn. "I want that, but is there a way to get there without having to go through such difficulty?"

I desperately wanted to be able to tell her that she would be the exception to what we find on so many pages of Scripture, but I couldn't. As I looked at her hesitancy, I could only guess at what her being upended would look like; even so, I wanted to say—joining with those other voices that day who had just given testimony—"It will be worth it; trust Jesus; you will know weakness unlike anything before, but he is strong and kind." She was scared, and who could blame her? But that was only because she had yet to experience the sufficiency of the grace. Jesus wants to give each of us a testimony to his grace—a grace that is greater than the greatest thorn.

This isn't just true for people coming to new life in Jesus; it is the ongoing experience of the Christian life. Biblical truth about his grace, which we may well have sung about countless times in hymns of worship, only becomes real to us as our lives testify to our need of this kind of Savior. The full power of his sufficient grace can only become precious to us in the crucible of our own inadequacy. The occasions will always be at uncomfortable moments when we come face-to-face with our weakness. We will be dying to ourselves and rising to new life, just as Jesus did in saving us. Our life and our lips will tell the story of the cross and resurrection. The Lord is working into each of us a life and testimony that can say with Paul, "For when I am weak, then I am strong" (2 Corinthians 12:10).

This is no mere pleasantry that Paul is tagging on to the story of his journey of "I prayed but nothing changed." It is the punch line. It is the great takeaway. This will be your testimony, too, so be filled with hope. I would like to have been a fly on the wall watching as the Corinthian congregation heard this punch line. Perhaps those who were new in faith politely acknowledged it, but were still so taken with the notion of being strong in themselves that they merely let it pass them by.

This is so often true of the modern church in the West. Despite our knowledge of the cross and Christ's victory through weakness, we are still surprised when the Lord invades our pursuit of worldly happiness in pursuit of an unsettling, but deeper, joy that can only be found in him. Yet had I been watching, would I have seen some Corinthian saints who had walked a bit further with Jesus, not just through mountaintop experiences but through the valleys of seemingly unanswered prayer, nodding their heads yes? Perhaps they could also recount their own testimonies of strength through weakness. Yes, the details of their thorns were different from Paul's thorn, but the trajectory would have been to the same destination.

Do you remember why you picked up this book? I suspect it has something to do with your fears that something in your life and walk of faith has gone wrong—you have prayed, but nothing has changed. Surely it isn't supposed to be this way? You have been questioning why God, who says he loves you, is doing nothing. But now, having gotten this far, are you beginning to see that, far from him doing nothing, he is working while you are waiting? He has not forgotten you, and in ways that may only become clear later, or even in eternity, he is giving you a testimony of his strength in the midst of your weakness—a testimony you will want to tell others and that, ultimately, you will be amazed that you are living out.

Your testimony may not be shared in worship, as the men and women did who were baptized at our church. But you will tell it to your own soul in moments when you are tempted to be puffed up in your own eyes or overrun by a love of worldly strength. And then, do not be surprised if, eventually, your testimony is one of comfort that is used to bring comfort to others (2 Corinthians 1:4).

YOUR TESTIMONY WILL ALSO BE "WHEN I AM WEAK, THEN I AM STRONG"

Paul tells his experience with the thorn, his own I-prayed-and-nothing-changed moment, to the Corinthian church to do more than tell them an interesting story. He shares it so that they, too, will expect to be on the same journey as Jesus works new life into them. Without it they will not become who Jesus has called them to be, they will not live based on the joy of their new life, they will not be any use for reaching a dying world, and they will set all their hopes on the here and now rather than be hungry for eternity.

I would like to help you to put your testimony together in a way that echoes Paul's movement toward "when I am weak, then I am strong." It will not be neat and tidy; it will be personal and messy. Yet it will be a precious testimony that leaves you and others with no doubt that there is only One who is strong. Remember, you are going in a new direction of travel, and it may be that you are still early on in the journey. But be encouraged that you will, by God's grace, find your way to that strange place of feeling weak but knowing strength.

Here are four indispensable elements for your testimony of how when you are weak, God makes you strong:

1. *It starts with a thorn*—something, anything, that leaves you desperately pleading for relief or release. Take a moment and think (or write down) how your thorn has beat you down and left you feeling that you have little hope and strength to go on. In what ways has it attacked your hopes for your life and your sense of self? How does it seem to be robbing you of a future and leaving you unable to cope? What magic button do you long for God to press that would ease or end your struggle?
2. *Then, a seeming silence from heaven*—how are you questioning God and doubting his goodness? What has this struggle revealed about who you expect God to be and what you expect him to do for you? What reasons have you offered to God for wanting him to fix things according to your

plan? What lies of Satan have gained traction in your heart as you fight for faith? Take a moment and think about (or write down) your disappointments with God's response to your pleading for change.

3. *Next, the Lord wooing you toward his sufficient grace*—what has he said to you about your new life in Christ that initially felt totally insufficient for what you are facing? What defenses did you set up against his words? Tell the story of how you softened to his gentle words of grace and truth about Christ. What parts of Scripture have become precious to you as you have endured little or no change in circumstances? Take a moment and think about (or write down) how God has been speaking to you.
4. *At last, an embrace of strength in weakness*—how has this process of weakening caused you to lean on Christ more than before? How has walking in weakness become less scary to you now? How has your appreciation of Christ's way of winning through weakness become more precious to you? How have letting go of your strength and living out of his strength fitted you to better serve like him? Take a moment and think about (or write down) how you are seeing Christ's strength in your weakness.

The Lord has written weakness into your life not to crush you but to find the end of the story as a testimony to his strength. It will be hard-won, and you will probably have to wait in hope to see all that he is doing. But make no mistake: while you are waiting, he is working. In his book *Waiting on God,* Andrew Murray explains,

> He is constantly seeking to win the heart of his child for himself. He wishes that we would not only say, when he bestows the gift, "How good is God!" but long before it comes, even if it never comes, we should all the time be experiencing; it is good that a man should quietly wait. The Lord is good unto them that wait.[1]

Does this kind of testimony feel out of reach for you? We don't usually expect to have a testimony of God's grace to share when our prayers seem to have changed nothing. That was certainly the case for Helen. She came to see me after the most turbulent year of her life. If you had met her before that year, you would have come to know her as a capable and lively young woman whose faith in Christ was vibrant. Her emotional resilience was often a source of strength for others, and she enjoyed providing a safe place for others with needs through her presence. Things changed for her after a deeply distressing event unfolded at her job as a healthcare professional. The things she experienced and witnessed left her with terrifying flashbacks, random panic attacks, and an emotional fragility that left her debilitated and ashamed. She wondered why God would let it happen and was confused and angry at being laid so low. She just wanted relief and a return to her previous situation, and she couldn't understand why God wasn't changing anything about this ongoing struggle. The fear that her ordeal would leave her permanently changed for the worse felt suffocating.

With the support of her pastor and a loving church, she was encouraged to connect with me for counseling. The last thing she expected was that she would have a testimony of God's grace. But this is the note she sent to me years later:

> It has been five years since the traumatic incident I came to see you about. I remember when I first came and you told me about a lady who had suffered greatly but was strangely thankful for the way it had helped her get to know Jesus better. I remember thinking that was crazy and I certainly never wanted to be that person. Yet, by God's grace, that is where I am today!
>
> Life is still really hard for so much of the time and I'm still the girl that cries a lot though church small group and in worship services. Yet, the way that I know the Lord is completely different. I have to pray for his help to get through the day, and I'm slowly learning to rely on him. I can now see his goodness in the rubbish stuff I've been through. On good days I see that maybe knowing him better is the best thing even though I may still feel awful.
>
> You pointed me to God's kindness that I couldn't see at the time. I know I wasn't a barrel of laughs, so thank you for showing some of God's patience in being patient with me.[2]

The Lord gave her a testimony not of answered prayer but of something even more powerful—a strength in the Lord that can only be found in feeling her weakness acutely. And now she no longer wants to live out of a renewed worldly strength with everything fixed, but instead wants to declare, "When I am weak, then I am strong." Her testimony has changed from when I first met her, when she determinedly and tearfully said, "I prayed and nothing changed," to where she is today, saying, "I prayed and everything changed."

LIVING LIFE "IN CHRIST"

One of my proudest achievements as a father of daughters is that I've been able to get through their younger years without ever having to sit through their favorite film, *Frozen* (or *Frozen 2* for that matter). Despite that, I am all too well aware of the main character, not least because of the number of Elsa costumes I have had to buy as gifts for the girls. My daughter Emily was particularly taken by the idea of being in everything Elsa. So she would wear Elsa pajamas at night, then immediately change into one of her several Elsa costumes the moment she got up.

Her imagination was overflowing with what it would mean to be in Elsa, and she was not slow to tell us how she expected to be treated when she was in Elsa. All the privileges and lifestyle of Elsa would be hers; after all, why not? She was in Elsa. She even tried freezing her younger sister once, and was quite surprised when it didn't work. But it all came to an end after attending a children's fancy dress-up party—you've guessed it—"in Elsa." She expected to be treated as Elsa, yet she was not. Her experience was nothing like being Elsa, and at that tender age, it made no sense why being in Elsa wouldn't mean she got treated like and had the same experience as the character she adored. She became disillusioned and gave up. It seems, though, that when we pray and nothing changes, then we become disillusioned and want to give up, it is for the opposite reason. We are surprised when we find we get treated like, and have the same kind of experiences as, Jesus.

Remember, Paul seems to think that knowing the new life you have in Christ is particularly important when trying to work out why your life is not going how you would want or expect: "If anyone is in Christ, the new creation has come: the old has gone, the new is here!" (2 Corinthians 5:17).

This is not make-believe dress-up. We have been objectively taken up to be "in Christ." On the one hand, this is amazingly wonderful news. All of his merits are now counted to us, and we get treated by the Father as he would treat his Son. "In Christ" we are as welcomed, honored, accepted, and secure as Jesus is.

On the other hand, being "in Christ" means that the pattern of his life will be the pattern of our lives. He submitted to being weak, unimpressive, and broken so that the strength of his grace might be at work in the world and in my life. If that is what his life was like, we also should expect that our lives will be constantly subject to feeling and experiencing weakness, so that the strength of God might be manifested powerfully in our lives. We will increasingly experience the honor of being crushed like Jesus so that we not only experience his strength in us but also he shows his strength through us.

Being in Christ—dressed up in his life—inevitably will mean we share in afflictions that echo his grief, his disappointment, his rejection, and his facing of false allegations and injustice. That was what made so many of the testimonies of Jesus on our church's baptism day so compelling. They were like a trail of breadcrumbs pointing to the beauty of Christ's life, death, and resurrection. He died and rose victorious. When he was weak, his strength was made all the more manifest.

Too often, when thorny situations come our way, we say, "If I am in Jesus, this shouldn't happen to me." We are so surprised that being in Christ could mean this—surely the opposite should be true. But, although we do not delight in afflictions, unmet desires, hurts, and disappointments, we do learn to delight in the honor of living for Christ's sake. Though this is hard to embrace at first, we see through the struggle to the sacred privilege of having his life worked into our lives.

> "That is why, for Christ's sake, I delight in weaknesses . . . " (2 Corinthians 12:10)

Paul's thorny experience has been radically transformed from an affliction he was desperate to be rid of to precious cargo that he has been entrusted to carry for the glory of Jesus. He is no longer terrified by his thorn and the accompanying experience of feeling weak, but sees these things as a precious calling that Jesus is present in and helping him to fulfill. And for that honor, he is strangely delighted.

This is constantly taking me by surprise. My default is to think that I will be most useful to Christ and be most fulfilled by being strong. But the Lord Jesus is determined to work weakness into my life so that he can let his life be manifest in mine.

I wish that I had come to grips with this reality before setting out to write this book. I wanted to write a book about a journey through unanswered prayer to help readers see something of God's often unseen relentless pursuit of us in and through thorny seasons. Little did I expect that I would have to live through several years of struggle, prayers that seemed to change nothing, and a total collapse of my confidence that I had anything to write that would be helpful to anyone.

I would never have considered writing had I known that it would become an occasion for emotional burnout, being given a required leave of absence from work, and wanting to give up on ministry altogether. I pleaded with the Lord to remove my weakness and give me the strength as I had defined it. At the same time, my selfish ambition to do something strong and admired (like the Corinthians) was dismantled before my eyes, and my resentment at weakness became increasingly apparent even to me. I was forced into doing real battle to believe that weakness is the way and that God's grace really is sufficient. No longer was I writing words for others. Now I had to learn these deep truths firsthand.

It has been the hardest season of my life. Yet, as I am emerging on the other side, I am finding myself strangely thankful that it has been so hard. Not only have I been forced to treasure the sufficiency of his grace more, but also I am genuinely learning to delight that my weakness will show more of the life of Jesus. No matter how much I may want to be strong, I am slowly surrendering to the fact that Jesus wants my weakness. He is positioning me to be empty of self-sufficiency, worldly confidence, and conceit. In my better moments, I delight that the life of Christ is being worked into me.

This confession takes me back nearly twenty years to when my wife, Jane, was emerging from a five-year battle with chronic fatigue. It had taken her from being a confident and vibrant young woman with seemingly boundless energy (one ministry leader nicknamed her Tigger because she was constantly bouncing around and getting things done) to being bedbound in the hospital, unable to do the most basic of daily tasks. Her chronic fatigue was accompanied by agonizing nerve pain and clinical depression.

We had prayed for a change, but month after month, and year after year, no change had come. Her energy being gone meant her sense of worth was gone—she could no longer be "a Tigger." She just wanted to be who she was before. Yet the Lord wanted her to live out her new life in Christ, fully dependent on him. I will never forget the tears that came to my eyes, having seen all that she had had to endure, when one evening, as we reflected together, she said, "I would not wish what I have been through on anyone, but even if I could, I wouldn't change it for the world. Jesus is more my life than he has ever been. He doesn't need my strength. He needs my weakness."

The power of her testimony gave me a renewed hope in Christ. But I also remember wondering whether that grace would have the same effect on me if I ever found myself broken and pleading. Would I say the same thing? I know the answer now. It is a resounding "Yes!"

Perhaps you are asking yourself the same question as you come to the end of this book. Can I tell you that, no matter how far away it may seem right now, you will, against all expectations, find yourself at a point where you, too, will say a resounding "Yes!" If you find that hard to believe, then stop reading right now, get alone with the Lord, and ask him, "Please, will you give me a testimony of 'when I am weak, then I am strong.'"

He promises to answer that prayer with a resounding "Yes!" His grace is sufficient. He is doing wonderful things even when it doesn't feel like it.

For others of you, as you read these stories of the Lord's strength meeting weakness, you may realize that you have not gone back to Jesus to remember and delight in what he has done and is doing in you and through you. Now is the time. Write your testimony or just think it through. Then think of who you can bring into your renewed joy. Who can you pass your story on to for the glory of Christ? As you become a living testimony, never doubt that the God of all comfort will be the one who always "comforts us in all our troubles, so that we can comfort those in any trouble with the comfort we ourselves receive from God" (2 Corinthians 1:4).

God's grace is sufficient, and will be sufficient, for all who call on Jesus's name.

ACKNOWLEDGMENTS

If there is any wisdom, clarity, or insight in these pages, it is because the God of grace delights to confound the wisdom of the world by speaking through weak, unimpressive, and dependent people. This book has been my undoing and, I pray, my redoing. To him alone goes the glory.

The context where I have lived this out, both painfully and with a sense of huge privilege, has been among my church family at Speke Baptist Church. I know of no other community that has loved me so well. Over many years they have given no quarter in any of my many attempts to think more of myself than I ought, yet, more so, they have given endless grace and patience as my shortcomings have become increasingly apparent. They have shown me Christ in so many more ways than I feel I have ever shown him to them. It is an honor to pastor these dear ones. The same is true for the countless others who have shared their stories with me as we have walked together for a while.

My mentors in the sacred ministry of ministering God's Word to souls of fellow strugglers are many, but none more so than the faculty, both past and present, of CCEF. Had I not, seemingly by accident, found myself studying their online courses, I wonder where my faith and ministry would be today. Their love, humility, and generosity have been used by the Lord to change my life in ways too numerable to mention—not only through study but also through welcoming me as an intern with them, getting to know them, and seeing Christ at work in them. A particular expression of gratitude goes to Mike and Jody Emlet, Ed and Sheri Welch, and Alasdair Groves for warmly making time to care for me when I was at my weakest. I owe you a debt of love that I cannot repay.

It was only ten years ago, spawned out of similar influences to CCEF, that Biblical Counselling (yes, two Ls) UK emerged. In many ways, the fellowship and shared experience of finding what the Lord would be doing among those of us who have contributed to the developing vision have given me a second church. Working on the certificate course, intern program, and conferences has sharpened me, but it has been the prayers, fellowship, and shared journey that mean the most to me. Thanks to you all. We are blessed to be led by Steve and Beth Midgley, whom I think of as my big brother and sister in the Lord. Their humility and loving wisdom have set an impeccable example for Jane and myself.

It is a understatement to say that I find writing a paralyzing experience, so it is not too much to say that this book project would have floundered long ago had it not been for the gracious expertise, long-suffering persistence, and disarming sense of humor of my editor, Barbara Juliani. When I was done and saw no hope, she picked me up, and over many hours, I was painstakingly walked through the baby steps of getting thoughts down through the keyboard. I have no desire to write any further books, but the only thing that might cause me to start typing again would be the prospect of working with her again. You have been a blessing to me.

Yet, while many have helped or influenced me in the writing of this book, only one person has actually had to live it all with me. That is my wife, Jane. She was faultless in her quiet support, while lesser women would have said, "Enough!" long ago. We have shared the highs and lows of "I prayed but nothing changed," and I have experienced the love and wisdom of Christ toward me through her. Only I will ever know how much my attention to the material, and the providences of living it out, have been a cost that she has had to carry. Yet, she has done so with amazing grace and faith, and I couldn't be more proud to call her my wife.

ENDNOTES

Chapter 1

1. C. S. Lewis, *A Grief Observed* (London: Faber, 1964), 26–27.

2. Timothy Keller, *Prayer* (London: Hodder and Stoughton, 2014), 3.

3. Jason Meyer, *Don't Lose Heart* (Grand Rapids: Baker Books, 2019), 30.

4. Jerry Sittser, *A Grace Revealed* (Grand Rapids: Zondervan, 2012), 19.

5. C. S. Lewis, *Mere Christianity* (New York: Macmillan, 1952), 53–54.

Chapter 2

1. Craig Groeschel, *Dangerous Prayers: Because Following Jesus Was Never Meant to Be Safe* (Grand Rapids: Zondervan, 2020), 33.

2. John Calvin, *Institutes of the Christian Religion: Volume 1*, ed. John T. McNeill, trans. Ford Lewis Battles (Louisville, KY: Westminster John Knox Press, 1960), 1:108.

Chapter 3

1. Jerry Sittser, *A Grace Revealed* (Grand Rapids: Zondervan, 2012), 80–81.

2. Joe Thorn, *Experiencing the Trinity: The Grace of God for the People of God* (Wheaton, IL: Crossway, 2015), 7.

3. John Piper, *Don't Waste Your Cancer* (Wheaton, IL: Crossway, 2011), 6.

4. Thomas A. Kempis, *The Imitation of Christ: Selections Annotated & Explained* (Nashville, TN: Turner Publishing Company, 2012), chap. 8.

5. Mike Emlet, "When It Won't Go Away: A Biblical Response to Chronic Pain," *Journal of Biblical Counseling* 23, no. 1 (2005; Christian Counseling and Educational Foundation, Glenside, PA).

6. Author uncertain, "How Firm a Foundation," in *Trinity Hymnal* (Suvanee, Great Commission Publications, 1990), 94.

7. Martha Snell Nicholson, "The Thorn," The Gospel Coalition, February 1, 2010, https://www.thegospelcoalition.org/blogs/justin-taylor/the-thorn/.

Chapter 4

1. Mark Vroegop, *Dark Clouds, Deep Mercy: Discovering the Grace of Lament* (Wheaton, IL: Crossway, 2019), 32.

2. C. S. Lewis, *The Magician's Nephew* (New York, NY: HarperCollins, 1983), 160.

3. Lewis, *The Magician's Nephew*, 168.

4. Pete Grieg, *God on Mute* (Colorado Springs, CO: David C. Cook, 2007), 50.

5. Timothy Keller, *Prayer: Experiencing Awe and Intimacy with God* (United Kingdom: Hodder & Stoughton, 2016), 25.

6. Michael S. Horton, *A Place For Weakness* (Grand Rapids, MI: Zondervan, 2010), 122.

Chapter 5

1. Paul David Tripp, "Talking to Yourself." Wednesday's Word. Last modified March 13, 2013, www.paultripp.com/wednesdays-word/posts/talking-to-yourself.

2. David Powlison, *Making All Things New* (Wheaton, IL: Crossway, 2017), 114–15.

Chapter 6

1. Paul David Tripp, "The Radical Implications of Eternity," 2010, Philadelphia Conference on Reformed Theology, Alliance of Confessing Evangelicals. MP3 download set.

2. David Mathis, *Habits of Grace: Enjoying Jesus through the Spiritual Disciplines* (Wheaton, IL: Crossway, 2016), 5.

3. Dane Ortlund, *Deeper: Real Change for Real Sinners*, Union (Wheaton, IL: Crossway, 2021), 44.

Chapter 7

1. Joni Eareckson Tada, "Joy Hard Won," *Decision*, March 2000, 12.

Chapter 8

1. Andrew Murray, *Waiting on God* (Radford, VA: Wilder, 2008), 64.

2. Note used with permission.